Business and Personal Law
Real-World Connections

Student Activity Workbook
with Academic Integration

 **Glencoe**

New York, New York   Columbus, Ohio   Chicago, Illinois   Woodland Hills, California

Glencoe

The *McGraw·Hill* Companies

Printed in the United States of America.

Send all inquires to:
Glencoe/McGraw-Hill
21600 Oxnard Street, Suite 500
Woodland Hills, CA 91367

ISBN: 978-0-07-877944-2   (Student Edition)
MHID: 0-07-877944-8   (Student Edition)

3 4 5 6 7 8 9   045   12 11 10 09 08

Table of Contents

Table of Contents

Contents

Table of Contents

Table of Contents

Table of Contents

Table of Contents

Table of Contents

Chapter 1 The Law and the Courts

Section 1.1 The Foundations of Law

 Note Taking

Directions As you read, write notes, facts, and main ideas in the Note Taking column. Write key words and short phrases in the Cues column. Then summarize the section in the Summary box.

Cues	Note Taking
• Morality: values about right and wrong	**ETHICS AND MORALITY** • People use different methods to decide on the right thing to do. **ETHICS AND LAW** • Following ethical rules helps deal with moral questions. Ethics are subjective, laws are objective. • Five main sources of U.S. law:

Summary

Laws are necessary and are created because people do not always do what they are supposed to do.

Chapter 1 The Law and the Courts

Section 1.1 The Foundations of Law

 Social Studies
Articles of the Constitution

Directions The U.S. Constitution was created to describe the three branches of government, to set limits within which the government may pass laws, and to define the rights of the people. Explain how each of the seven Articles accomplishes this by writing your answers on the lines provided.

1. Article I

_____

_____

2. Article II

_____

_____

3. Article III

_____

_____

4. Article IV

_____

_____

5. Article V

_____

_____

6. Article VI

_____

_____

7. Article VII

_____

_____

Chapter 1 The Law and the Courts
Section 1.1 The Foundations of Law

 Study Skills
Paraphrasing

Directions Read the box below. Then read each paragraph that follows and paraphrase it on the lines provided.

PARAPHRASING
Paraphrasing means restating a main idea in your own words. It helps you learn to take notes as you read. Paraphrasing helps you focus on the main idea and not get bogged down by all the details. When you paraphrase a reading passage, you do the following: • Distinguish between important and unimportant information. • Use your own words to write down the main idea. • Use words and phrases instead of sentences.

The Golden Rule says, "Do unto others as you would have them do unto you." Many people prefer this rule because it works in many situations. The heart of the Golden Rule is empathy. Empathy means putting yourself in another person's position. One way to test whether an action is right or wrong under the Golden Rule is to ask, "Would I want to be treated this way?" If your answer is no, then the action breaks the Golden Rule.

_____

_____

_____

_____

In the early days of England's history, the king tried to centralize the English court system. Judges traveled around the country deciding cases. Because there was no written law, judges made decisions based on the customs and traditions of the people. Judges shared their decisions with one another so that the same laws would be applied everywhere in the country. This practice formed the basis of common law.

_____

_____

_____

_____

Chapter 1 The Law and the Courts

Section 1.1 The Foundations of Law

 Test Taking
Multiple-Choice Tests

Directions Read the tips below. Then fill in the circle next to the word or phrase that best answers each question.

MULTIPLE-CHOICE TEST TIPS
• Read each answer choice carefully. • Eliminate the choices you know are incorrect. • For each remaining choice, ask yourself if it is a good answer or not a good answer. • Be careful. An answer choice may be a true statement, but not the best answer to the question.

1. What do you call the values that govern a group's ideas about right and wrong?
   ○ ethics
   ○ morality
   ○ opinions
   ○ greatest good

2. What do you call the moral rules that most people know without thinking about them?
   ○ real-world ethics
   ○ character traits
   ○ opinions
   ○ integrity

3. Laws are created to do all of the following except
   ○ define the legal rights and responsibilities of the people.
   ○ require certain actions or forbid others.
   ○ instill personal values and views on ethics and morality.
   ○ enforce the rights and duties of people through the police.

4. Which of the following is not one of the five main sources of U.S. law?
   ○ court decisions
   ○ common law
   ○ morality
   ○ statutes

5. A past case that a court follows when making a present decision is called
   ○ common law.
   ○ a precedent.
   ○ civil law.
   ○ a statute.

Chapter 1 The Law and the Courts
Section 1.2 The Court System and Trial Procedures

 Note Taking

Directions As you read, write notes, facts, and main ideas in the Note Taking column. Write key words and short phrases in the Cues column. Then summarize the section in the Summary box.

Cues	Note Taking
• Two U.S. court systems: federal and state	**FEDERAL AND STATE COURT SYSTEMS** • Federal courts hear cases with federal subjects and cases involving people from different states or another country. **CIVIL TRIAL PROCEDURE** • Civil law governs the relationships between two individual parties. **CRIMINAL TRIAL PROCEDURE** • Criminal cases begin with an arrest.

Summary
The federal and state courts are divided into various levels.

Chapter 1 The Law and the Courts

Section 1.2 The Court System and Trial Procedures

English Language Arts
Compare and Contrast

Directions Civil court cases and criminal court cases have different purposes and procedures. Complete the chart to compare and contrast the two types of court cases. The first one has been done for you.

Civil Court Cases	Criminal Court Cases
Used to govern the relationships between two individual parties	Used to determine if a person committed a crime
	Are brought by the government
	Can be settled only through the courts
Can be tried by a jury or a judge	
	Lawyers begin trial with opening statements, present evidence, give closing statements, and jury or judge renders a decision.
Decision of jury may not need to be unanimous.	
	If defendant is found guilty, defendant is sentenced.
Judgment of the court must be carried out, or executed.	
A lower court decision can be appealed to a higher court.	

Chapter 1 The Law and the Courts
Section 1.2 The Court System and Trial Procedures

 Study Skills
Using Reading Strategies

Directions Read the tips below. For each numbered heading that follows, restate each into a question. Then answer the questions based on the text. The first one has been done for you.

TIPS FOR READING TEXT	
Preread	• Think about what you already know. • Read the chapter title, section titles, section opening pages (Reading Guide, What You'll Learn, Why It's Important), all headings, and summary for each chapter. • Look at the visuals. Read the captions.
Question	• Ask questions as you read each heading. • Change each heading into one or more questions. Use the words *who, what, when, where, why,* or *how* in your question. • Write the questions in your study notebook. • Leave space for the answers.
Read	• Read your text to find the answers to the questions you asked.
Write	• In your notebook, write the answer under each question.

1. Courts of Appeals

   What are courts of appeals? They are courts that hear appeals and review cases from the lower

   courts. _____

2. Juvenile Courts

   _____

   _____

3. Alternative Dispute Resolution

   _____

   _____

4. Remedies

   _____

   _____

5. Arraignment

   _____

   _____

Chapter 1 The Law and the Courts

Section 1.2 The Court System and Trial Procedures

Test Taking
Reducing Test Anxiety

Directions Read the tips below. Then answer the questions that follow by writing the correct answer in the space provided.

TIPS FOR REDUCING TEST ANXIETY
• Avoid talking to other students about the test. Saying you are scared—or hearing others say they are scared—causes more anxiety.
• Take three deep breaths as you begin the test and whenever you feel anxiety during the test.
• Concentrate on one test question at a time. If you lose your concentration, do not panic. Breathe and bring your focus back to the question.

1. Which of the following is not part of the federal court system?
   a. district courts   **c.** courts of appeals
   b. juvenile courts   **d.** Supreme Court

   _____

2. Why does the Supreme Court decide to hear a case?
   a. two of the nine justices decide to hear the case
   b. the Chief Justice decides to hear the case
   c. lower courts disagree on how to resolve the case
   d. the President of the United States refers the case to the Supreme Court

   _____

3. What are the time limits for when a plaintiff may sue a defendant called?
   a. statutes of limitation   **c.** litigation
   b. survival statutes   **d.** arbitration

   _____

4. What is conciliation?
   a. a negotiation where each party appoints a person as a representative
   b. a negotiation where the intermediary brings the parties together
   c. a negotiation where only the intermediary makes the final decision
   d. a negotiation where the intermediary meets separately with the parties involved

   _____

5. Which is not a step in a trial?
   a. selecting a jury   **c.** arbitration
   b. arguments and evidence   **d.** verdict and judgment

   _____

Chapter 1 The Law and the Courts
Chapter Content Vocabulary
 English Language Arts
Writing

Directions Select ten words from the list below. Use each in a sentence that shows you understand the meaning of the word.

administrative law	bail	jurisdiction
alternative dispute resolution (ADR)	common law	justice
appellate court	constitution	law
arraignment	detention hearing	morality
arrest	ethics	statute

1. _____

   _____

2. _____

   _____

3. _____

   _____

4. _____

   _____

5. _____

   _____

6. _____

   _____

7. _____

   _____

8. _____

   _____

9. _____

   _____

10. _____

    _____

Chapter 1

Chapter 1 The Law and the Courts
Chapter Academic Vocabulary

 English Language Arts
Reading Skills

Directions Circle the letter of the phrase that best completes each sentence.

1. **Empathy** means
   a. to apply to many situations.
   b. to lie to save somebody's life.
   c. to put yourself in another person's position.
   d. to know without thinking.

2. Telling a lie to save a person's life might be considered **permissible**, or
   a. acceptable.
   b. dangerous.
   c. wrong.
   d. unethical.

3. In Europe, the civil law system is **prevalent**, or
   a. immoral.
   b. unlawful.
   c. never used.
   d. used widely.

4. In juvenile courts, hearings are **informal**, which means they
   a. are open to the general public.
   b. are more casual and less formal.
   c. do not protect the privacy of minors.
   d. are not attended by the juvenile offender.

5. A **mediator**
   a. is hired by the parties to settle a dispute.
   b. tries to persuade the parties to compromise.
   c. represents each party to try to hammer out an agreement.
   d. goes back and forth between parties to seek a consensus.

6. According to the principle of double **jeopardy**, a person who is found not guilty
   a. may request a second trial.
   b. cannot be tried twice for the same crime in the same kind of court.
   c. may be fined twice the amount.
   d. cannot ever receive the death penalty.

Chapter 2 Criminal Law
Section 2.1 Crimes and Criminal Justice
 Note Taking

Directions As you read, write notes, facts, and main ideas in the Note Taking column. Write key words and short phrases in the Cues column. Then summarize the section in the Summary box.

Chapter 2

Cues	Note Taking
• Felony: major crime, punishable by fine or imprisonment, sometimes death	**CLASSIFICATIONS OF CRIMES** • A crime is an offense committed against the public good, or society. **CRIMINAL LAW** • The U.S. legal system is made up of the federal court system and the state court system. **ELEMENTS OF A CRIME** • A crime has two elements: the criminal act and the required state of mind. **DEFENSES TO CRIMES** • Defendants can use several defenses to explain their actions.

Summary
Criminal laws in the United States are very specific because the offenses and punishment are very serious.

Chapter 2 Criminal Law

Section 2.1 Crimes and Criminal Justice

 Reading Comprehension
Classification

Directions Classifying information helps you remember important details.
There are three classifications of crimes in the United States. Complete the
chart to describe each classification. Provide the punishment and at least one
example for each type of crime.

Felony	Misdemeanor	Infraction
Definition: _____ _____ _____ _____	Definition: _____ _____ _____ _____	Definition: _____ _____ _____ _____
Punishment: _____ _____ _____ _____	Punishment: _____ _____ _____ _____	Punishment: _____ _____ _____ _____
Example(s): _____ _____ _____ _____	Example(s): _____ _____ _____ _____	Example(s): _____ _____ _____ _____

Chapter 2 Criminal Law
Section 2.1 Crimes and Criminal Justice

 Study Skills
Improving Concentration

Directions Read the tips below. Then answer the questions that follow. If the statement is true, circle the letter *T*. If the statement is false, circle the letter *F* and write the correct version on the lines provided.

TIPS FOR IMPROVING CONCENTRATION
• Improving your concentration allows you to take in more information at a faster rate.
• Go to your study place. Remove all distractions: turn off the phone and the television.
• Plan to study for 20 minutes, then take a break. Repeat this throughout your study period.
• Before you begin, take a couple of deep breaths. Say these words in your head as you breathe in: "I breathe in and let go of my thoughts." As you breathe out, say: "I breathe out and relax."
• As you study, remind yourself to think about what you are reading. You may be able to concentrate for only a few moments before other thoughts start coming into your mind. Do not give up. Concentration takes practice. Before you know it, you will be able to concentrate for longer and longer periods of time.

1. The government official who brings a case against a defendant is called the prosecutor.   T   F

_____

_____

2. The power to create the Federal Bureau of Investigation comes from a special clause in the Constitution called Article IV.   T   F

_____

_____

3. Motive is all that is needed to prove that a defendant committed a crime.   T   F

_____

_____

4. Some criminal laws make not doing something a crime.   T   F

_____

_____

Chapter 2 Criminal Law
Section 2.1 Crimes and Criminal Justice

Test Taking
What to Do During a Test

Directions Read the tips below. Then answer the questions that follow.

WHAT TO DO DURING A TEST
• Read the directions carefully first. • Budget the time you have for taking the test. • Change your seating position to help you relax. • If you do not know an answer, skip it and go on. • If your mind goes blank during an essay test, start writing notes on the topic. Ideas and answers will come to you. • Do not worry if others finish the test before you do. Stick to your budgeted time. • If you have time, go back to any answers you skipped. Mark an answer, even if it is your best guess. Double-check your answers.

1. What are some strategies for budgeting your time during a test?

_____

_____

_____

2. What are some strategies for helping you relax during a test?

_____

_____

_____

3. What are some strategies to use when your mind goes blank on a question?

_____

_____

_____

4. What are some strategies to use if you have time left at the end of a test?

_____

_____

_____

Chapter 2

Chapter 2 Criminal Law
Section 2.2 Types of Crimes

 Note Taking

Directions As you read, write notes, facts, and main ideas in the Note Taking column. Write key words and short phrases in the Cues column. Then summarize the section in the Summary box. Use an extra sheet of paper if necessary.

Cues	Note Taking
• Murder: intentional killing of another person	**TYPES OF CRIMES** • Categories of crimes: crimes against people, property, business, government, society

Summary

Crimes can affect people, property, business, government, and society.

Chapter 2

Chapter 2 Criminal Law

Section 2.2 Types of Crimes

 Mathematics
Reading a Table

Directions In May, 56,146 felony cases were filed in the 75 largest U.S. counties. Study the table below. Then answer the questions that follow. Round off your answers as needed.

Violent Crimes	Percent
Assault	12.7
Robbery	5.4
Rape	1.8
Murder	0.8
Other	4.3
Other Crimes	**Percent**
Drug trafficking	17.1
Other drug offenses	18.6
Theft	8.8
Burglary	8.1

1. What was the total percentage of violent crimes during May? _____

2. Based on your answer to question 1, how many of the 56,146 cases were violent crimes?

   _____

3. How many crimes were robberies?

   _____

4. What was the total percentage of Other Crimes? _____

5. Based on your answer to question 4, how many of the 56,146 cases were Other Crimes?

   _____

6. How many crimes were drug trafficking?

   _____

7. How many were burglaries? _____

Chapter 2 Criminal Law

Section 2.2 Types of Crimes

Study Skills
Learning New Material

Directions Read the tips below. Then answer the questions that follow.

TIPS FOR LEARNING NEW MATERIAL
• Preview the material by scanning the table of contents, headings, and photo captions.   • Decide on your intention by thinking about what you want to learn from the material.   • Break up the material into smaller units.   • After reading each unit, explain the information in your own words.   • Reread any sections that are not clear to you.

1. Scan Section 2.2: Types of Crimes. List what features are in the section.

_____

_____

_____

2. What should your intention be in reading the section again?

_____

_____

_____

3. How would you break this section into smaller units to make it easier to read?

_____

_____

_____

4. Read the section again. Write a short summary of each smaller unit you created in question 3.

_____

_____

_____

5. Did this Study Skills strategy help you better comprehend what you read in the section? Why or why not?

_____

_____

_____

Chapter 2 Criminal Law

Section 2.2 Types of Crimes

 Test Taking
Multiple-Choice Questions

Directions Read the tips below. Then answer the questions that follow by writing the correct answer in the space provided.

MULTIPLE-CHOICE QUESTION TIPS
Multiple-choice items on standardized tests consist of a stem, or question, and distractors, or answer choices. Often, test takers read the stem, glance at the distractors, and quickly choose the answer they think is right. A better test-taking strategy is to read the stem and each distractor carefully before deciding. If you are unsure of the answer, eliminate distractors you know are not correct before deciding among the remaining choices.

1. Which of the following is not a category of crime?
   a. crimes against people
   b. crimes against the government
   c. crimes against animals
   d. crimes against society

   _____

2. Which of the following is a crime against people?
   a. assault
   b. burglary
   c. shoplifting
   d. rioting

   _____

3. Which of the following is not a crime against property?
   a. vandalism
   b. burglary
   c. rioting
   d. larceny

   _____

4. What is the unlawful taking of someone's property with the intent of keeping it from that person?
   a. vandalism
   b. burglary
   c. larceny
   d. robbery

   _____

5. What is the act of engaging in deception to obtain money or property?
   a. bribery
   b. embezzlement
   c. forgery
   d. fraud

   _____

Chapter 2 Criminal Law
Chapter Content Vocabulary

 English Language Arts
Writing

Directions Write one or two sentences for each word to show that you understand the word's meaning. The first one has been done for you.

1. crime ___A person who is accused of a **crime** has the right to defend himself or herself.___
_____

2. felony _____
_____

3. misdemeanor _____
_____

4. manslaughter _____
_____

5. battery _____
_____

6. assault _____
_____

7. larceny _____
_____

8. robbery _____
_____

9. vandalism _____
_____

10. infraction _____
_____

11. defendant _____
_____

12. prosecutor _____
_____

Chapter 2 Criminal Law

Chapter Academic Vocabulary

 English Language Arts
Reading Skills

Directions Fill in the chart with the best word from the list below. Then use the word in a sentence. The first one has been done for you.

domestic	motive
intent	contempt
malicious	impulse

A purpose or plan to commit a crime **1.** The police were convinced his intent was to steal money.	intent
A reason that explains why a defendant committed an act **2.** _____ _____	
A sudden feeling that makes someone want to do something **3.** _____ _____	
Having to do with the home or family **4.** _____ _____	
Having or showing a feeling of wanting to hurt or harm someone **5.** _____ _____	
Showing a lack of respect in court **6.** _____ _____	

Chapter 3 Tort Law

Section 3.1 Definition of a Tort

 Note Taking

Directions As you read, write notes, facts, and main ideas in the Note Taking column. Write key words and short phrases in the Cues column. Then summarize the section in the Summary box.

Cues	Note Taking
• Victim/innocent party/ person injured: plaintiff	**TORT LAW** • A tort is a wrong committed against a person or property.

Summary
A tort is different from a crime.

Name _____ Date _____ Class _____

Chapter 3 Tort Law
Section 3.1 Definition of a Tort

 Reading Comprehension
Compare and Contrast

Directions Tort law in the United States has similarities to and differences
from tort law in Mexico. In the Venn diagram below, list what is similar, what is
different, and what is found in both countries.

United States   **Both**   **Mexico**

U.S. law holds people
accountable.

Hold people
responsible for injury
and damage to others.

Mexican culture
holds people accountable.

Chapter 3 Tort Law

Section 3.1 Definition of a Tort

Study Skills
Mind Maps

Directions Use the tips below to help improve your reading comprehension. Then complete the mind map that follows.

MIND MAPS
Mind maps are a good way to organize related pieces of information. In the center circle, write the main idea of the passage. In the outer circles, write details that support or explain the main idea. Follow these steps: **1.** Skim the passage and look for the most important idea. **2.** Write a word or phrase about the main idea in the center circle. **3.** Skim the passage again and look for concepts and details that support the main idea. **4.** Write these concepts or details in the outer circles. **5.** Carefully read the passage. **6.** Revise your mind map by adding clarity and details. Add more spokes and circles if necessary.

INTERNATIONAL TORTS AGAINST PERSONS

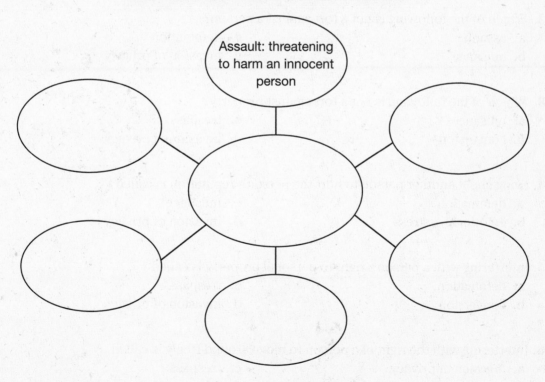

Chapter 3

Chapter 3 Tort Law
Section 3.1 Definition of a Tort

 **Test Taking**
Managing Stress

Directions Read the box below. Then answer the questions that follow by circling the letter of the correct answer.

MANAGING STRESS
Most students experience some kind of stress during tests. The stress you experience can have real physical manifestations. Depending on the severity, you may sweat, breathe harder, feel confused, or be unable to concentrate.   Stress is a natural reaction and can be properly managed. In fact, stress can actually help you do better. A key to managing stress is to focus and answer one question at a time. If you find your mind wandering, focus by looking up, breathing deeply, and then refocusing on the task at hand.

1. The purpose of tort law is to
   a. protect society from criminals.
   b. limit the rights of criminals.
   c. compensate the victim.
   d. interfere with a person's rights.

2. Which of the following is not a tort against a person?
   a. assault
   b. nuisance
   c. defamation
   d. invasion of privacy

3. Which of the following is not a tort against property?
   a. nuisance
   b. conversion
   c. trespass
   d. invasion of privacy

4. Lying about another person to hurt the person's reputation is called
   a. defamation
   b. emotional distress
   c. nuisance
   d. invasion of privacy

5. Interfering with a person's right to personal property is called
   a. defamation.
   b. conversion.
   c. trespass.
   d. invasion of privacy.

6. Interfering with the right of a person to move around freely is called
   a. invasion of privacy.
   b. conversion.
   c. trespass.
   d. false imprisonment.

Chapter 3 Tort Law

Section 3.2 Negligence and Liability

 Note Taking

Directions As you read, write notes, facts, and main ideas in the Note Taking column. Write key words and short phrases in the Cues column. Then summarize the section in the Summary box.

Cues	Note Taking
• Duty of care: obligation to use reasonable care	**NEGLIGENCE** • Negligence: accidental tort resulting when one person carelessly injures another • Elements of negligence: duty of care owed, duty breached by being careless, carelessness as proximate cause of harm, plaintiff hurt by carelessness • Defenses to negligence: **STRICT LIABILITY** • Some activities are so dangerous, liability always follows any injury from them.

Summary
Negligence occurs when one person carelessly injures another.

Chapter 3 Tort Law

Section 3.2 Negligence and Liability

 Social Studies
Analytical Skills

Directions Read the chart below. Then read the case studies that follow. In each case study, the tort suit was not successful. Write the reason why on the lines provided.

Element of Negligence	Definition
Duty of care	Obligation to use reasonable care
Breach of duty	Failure to use reasonable care
Proximate cause	Link between negligent conduct and injury strong enough to be recognized by law
Actual harm	Victim must have suffered injury, property loss, loss of money

Defense Against Negligence	Definition
Contributory negligence	Victim did something to help cause the injury
Comparative negligence	Carelessness of both parties weighed against each other
Assumption of risk	Plaintiff knew the risk but took the chance of being injured

1. A construction company dug a hole to repair a leak in a sewer line. The company posted warning signs and roped off the area with orange cones and yellow tape. A man walking through the area twisted his ankle severely when he stepped on a rock. He had to pay for his medical care and lost several days of work. The man sued the construction company for negligence.

   _____

   _____

2. A woman went bungee jumping for the first time. She was told it was dangerous but could be done successfully by following the safety rules and procedures. She paid the fee and received instructions on how to safely perform the sport. The elastic bungee cord was attached to her and she jumped. At the bottom, the cord pulled her back up into the air. This caused her head to snap back, injuring her neck. She sued for negligence.

   _____

   _____

Chapter 3 Tort Law

Section 3.2 Negligence and Liability

 Study Skills
Preparing a Place to Study

Directions Read the tips below. Then answer the questions that follow by making a check mark (✓) for each "yes" answer. If you cannot answer "yes" to each question, you may need to improve your study area.

STUDY PLACE TIPS
• Create a place where you can be alone. • Ask family members to leave you alone during your study time. • Make sure your study place is quiet. • Put all your study materials in your study place. • Add a desk or tabletop to your study place. • Make storage space for your books and materials. • Make sure your study place is well lit. • Make sure your study place is a comfortable temperature.

Question	Yes!
Can I be alone in my study place whenever I need to study?	
Do people respect my study time and leave me alone?	
Is my study place quiet?	
Are all my study materials in my study place?	
Is there a desk or tabletop I can use in my study place?	
Is there storage space for my books and materials in my study place?	
Is my study place well lit?	
Is the temperature comfortable in my study place?	

How can I make my study place better so that I can study business and personal law?

_____

_____

_____

_____

_____

_____

_____

Chapter 3

Chapter 3 Tort Law

Section 3.2 Negligence and Liability

 Test Taking
True/False Tests

Directions Read the tips below. Then answer the questions that follow by circling *T* for true or *F* for false.

TRUE/FALSE TEST TIPS
• In order for an answer to be true, every part of the sentence must be true. Even if there are true statements in the sentence, if any part is false, the answer cannot be true.
• If a statement contains negative words such as *no, not,* or *cannot,* drop the negative word and read the sentence again. If the sentence is then true, the answer is false.
• Sentences with words such as *sometimes, often, frequently, ordinarily,* and *generally* are often true. These words make a statement more likely to reflect something true.
• Absolute words such as *no, never, none, always, every,* and *only* usually indicate that every part of the sentence must be completely true. Often, sentences with these words are false.

1. Negligence is always a crime. It results when one person carelessly injures another. **T F**

2. Negligence is being less careful than a reasonable person should be in the same situation. **T F**

3. The law of torts is never grounded in the concept of a person's rights. **T F**

4. The reasonable person test is an objective test. It always changes because the injured party changes. **T F**

5. If a victim was not actually harmed, there can be negligence. **T F**

6. Strict liability is a legal doctrine that says that some activities are so dangerous that liability will always follow any injury that results from those activities. **T F**

7. When people are injured by defective products, fault always matters. **T F**

8. Product liability has no limits. **T F**

Chapter 3 Tort Law
Chapter Content Vocabulary
 English Language Arts
Definitions

Directions Match each word or phrase with its definition. Write the letter on the line next to the matching definition.

a. tort
b. tortfeasor
c. intentional tort
d. negligence
e. proximate cause
f. contributory negligence
g. comparative negligence
h. assumption of risk
i. strict liability

1. _____ A person who commits a tort

2. _____ Actions that hurt, embarrass, or scare other people

3. _____ A legal doctrine that says some activities are so dangerous that liability will always follow any injury that results from those activities

4. _____ A link between negligent conduct and injury strong enough to be recognized by law

5. _____ A tort that results when one person carelessly injures another

6. _____ A defense against negligence when the defense can show the victim contributed to the cause of the injury

7. _____ A wrong committed by one person against another

8. _____ A defense against negligence when the carelessness of each party is compared to the other's

9. _____ A defense against negligence raised when the plaintiff knew of the risk involved and still took the chance of being injured

Chapter 3 Tort Law

Chapter Academic Vocabulary

 English Language Arts
Reading Skills

Directions Complete each sentence by writing the letter of the word that correctly completes the sentence.

   a. compensate
   b. distress
   c. confidential
   d. reasonable
   e. objective
   f. foreseeable

1. The reasonable person test is a(n) _____ test that does not change because the injured party changes.

2. The court could not determine whether the injury was _____ at the time of the negligent conduct.

3. Sometimes one person can cause great emotional or mental _____ to another person, even if there is no intent to physically hurt the other person.

4. The purpose of tort law is to _____ the victim for injuries caused by the tortfeasor.

5. Negligence is being less careful than a(n) _____ person should be in the same situation.

6. People who use _____ records have to be careful to protect the privacy of the people related to those records.

Chapter 4 What Is a Contract?

Section 4.1 Agreements and Contracts

 Note Taking

Directions As you read, write notes, facts, and main ideas in the Note Taking column. Write key words and short phrases in the Cues column. Then summarize the section in the Summary box.

Cues	Note Taking
• Offer: proposal by one party to another to create a legal agreement	**CONTRACT LAW** • A contract is any agreement enforceable by law.

Summary

Contracts are created wherever people exchange things of value. They are not always written documents.

Chapter 4

Chapter 4 What Is a Contract?
Section 4.1 Agreements and Contracts

Reading Comprehension
Drawing Conclusions

Directions Study the list of types of contracts below. Read the situations that follow. Decide what type of contract each situation describes. Write the type on the line provided. Some situations can be more than one type of contract.

TYPES OF CONTRACTS	
bilateral	unilateral
express	valid
implied	void
oral	written
unenforceable	

_____ 1. A man went to a ski resort and paid $50 for a lift ticket. The cashier took the money and gave him a lift ticket. The man skied at the resort all day.

_____ 2. A woman asks a contractor to replace her driveway. The contractor gives her an estimate and contract. The terms include payment in full to the contractor when the job is completed. The woman agrees to hire the contractor and signs the contract.

_____ 3. An art gallery owner calls a local artist on the phone. The owner asks the artist if she would be willing to sell her paintings through the gallery. The artist says yes and agrees to supply the gallery with two paintings to sell.

_____ 4. Two months later, the same artist calls the gallery. She asks the owner if her two paintings have sold. The owner tells her no. The artist becomes upset and asks for the paintings back. The gallery owner agrees and sends them back to the artist.

_____ 5. A local government agency needs to purchase 35 new road signs. The agency is required by law to get three bids for contracts. A sign manufacturer guarantees the agency that it will match or beat any price given by its competitors. The agency buys the signs from this manufacturer without getting other bids.

Chapter 4 What Is a Contract?

Section 4.1 Agreements and Contracts

 Study Skills
Categorizing

Directions When you study, it is helpful to categorize information. This helps you organize terms and facts into distinct main ideas. Complete the chart that follows by placing each term under its appropriate category below.

acceptance	offer
bilateral	oral
capacity	unenforceable
consideration	unilateral
express	valid
genuine agreement	void
implied	voidable
legality	written

Contract Elements	Contract Characteristics

Chapter 4

Chapter 4 What Is a Contract?

Section 4.1 Agreements and Contracts

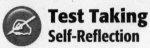

Test Taking
Self-Reflection

Directions On the lines below, write what you know about taking tests. Include any anecdotes or personal stories about how you handled stress or time management. Then identify your strengths and weaknesses in test taking and how you could improve. Write these in the chart that follows. Share your findings with a friend or classmate.

What I already know about taking tests:

_____

_____

_____

_____

_____

_____

_____

_____

_____

_____

_____

_____

Strengths	Weaknesses

Chapter 4

Chapter 4 What Is a Contract?

Section 4.2 How a Contract Begins

 Note Taking

Directions As you read, write notes, facts, and main ideas in the Note Taking column. Write key words and short phrases in the Cues column. Then summarize the section in the Summary box.

Cues	Note Taking
• Offeror: person making an offer	**OFFER** • An offer has three requirements: serious intent, definiteness and certainty, communication to offeree. **ACCEPTANCE** • An acceptance must be unconditional and follow the rules regarding the method of acceptance. **TERMINATION** • Five ways to terminate an offer: revocation, rejection, counteroffer, expiration of time, death, or insanity • Two important rules for revocation:

Summary
An offer is a proposal from one party to another.

Chapter 4

Chapter 4 What Is a Contract?

Section 4.2 How a Contract Begins

Reading Comprehension
Compare and Contrast

Directions Entering into a contract in the United States is different from entering into a contract in China. Complete the chart below to explain the similarities and differences. Then write a paragraph or two explaining the advantages and disadvantages of the two systems.

CONTRACTS IN THE UNITED STATES AND CHINA	
United States	**China**
Contracts are signed by all parties.	
All parties know who will do what, with what level of quality, and by what deadline.	
	Once contract is signed, parties know that activities may not happen as planned.

_____
_____
_____
_____
_____
_____
_____
_____
_____
_____
_____
_____
_____
_____

Chapter 4 What Is a Contract?

Section 4.2 How a Contract Begins

 Study Skills
Making a Plan to Learn

Directions Read the tips below. Then complete the graphic organizer that
follows as you reread Chapter 4.

RECORDING WHAT YOU KNOW AND LEARNED
Before you read a chapter, scan the chapter title and heads. Ask yourself, "What do I already know about this topic?" Write down your answers. Then ask, "What do I want to find out about the topic? What questions do I have about it?" Write down your answers. Read the chapter. As you read, take notes on important new information you did not think of or know about. Then write a summary combining what you knew with what you learned.

| What I Know | What I Want to Find Out
Questions I Have | Summary of What I
Learned |
| --- | --- | --- |
| | | |

Chapter 4

Chapter 4 What Is a Contract?

Section 4.2 How a Contract Begins

Test Prep
Using the "Be Here Now!" Strategy

Directions Read the box below and answer the questions that follow.

STAYING FOCUSED DURING A TEST
The ability to concentrate during a test is one of the keys to getting consistently high scores. You will do better if you are rested, well fed, and comfortable on test day. You can improve your ability to focus and concentrate by using the "Be here now!" strategy. If you find your mind wandering, say to yourself, "Be here now!" to bring your attention back to the task at hand. Do not judge your progress as you work through a test. If you find yourself worrying that you are doing poorly, use the "Be here now!" strategy to get back on track.

1. What are the three basic requirements to an offer?

   _____

   _____

2. How is an offer different from an invitation to negotiate?

   _____

   _____

3. What is the mirror image rule?

   _____

   _____

4. What is a counteroffer?

   _____

   _____

5. What is the difference between revocation and rejection?

   _____

   _____

Chapter 4 What Is a Contract?

Chapter Content Vocabulary

 English Language Arts
Definitions

Directions Circle the letter of the phrase that best completes the sentence.

1. **Contract** refers to
   a. a proposal by one party to another.
   b. a willingness to go along with another party.
   c. an agreement enforceable by law.
   d. an invitation to deal or trade.

2. **Acceptance** refers to
   a. a willingness to go along with a proposal.
   b. a proposal by one party to another.
   c. an invitation to deal or trade.
   d. an agreement enforceable by law.

3. A **genuine agreement** means that
   a. a valid acceptance is met by an invalid offer.
   b. an invalid offer is met by a valid acceptance.
   c. a valid offer is met by an invalid acceptance.
   d. a valid offer is met by a valid acceptance.

4. A **bilateral contract** is one that
   a. contains a promise by one person only.
   b. contains two promises.
   c. comes from the actions of the parties.
   d. is required to be written.

5. An **invitation to negotiate** is
   a. the same as an offer.
   b. the same as an acceptance.
   c. not an offer.
   d. legally binding.

6. To **counteroffer** is to
   a. reject all the terms of the original offer.
   b. take back an original offer.
   c. accept the terms of the original offer.
   d. change the terms of the original offer.

7. **Revocation** refers to
   a. the taking back of an offer.
   b. voiding an offer.
   c. accepting an offer.
   d. making another offer.

8. The **mirror image rule** states that
   a. the terms in an offer are void.
   b. the terms in an acceptance must match the terms in the original offer.
   c. a counteroffer must reflect the terms of an offer.
   d. the terms of an acceptance must be unilateral.

Chapter 4

Chapter 4 What Is a Contract?

Chapter Academic Vocabulary

 English Language Arts
Reading Skills

Directions Unscramble the letters of each term and write the correct term on the corresponding lines to the right. Then write the letter of the correct term after its definition in the list that follows.

a. cifyesp

b. pimsoe

c. rirueqe

d. niftiede

e. suasem

f. retnimede

a. _____

b. _____

c. _____

d. _____

e. _____

f. _____

1. to mention or tell in detail _____

2. to order, command, or insist on _____

3. to reach a decision after thought and investigation _____

4. to take on a certain look, form, or role _____

5. to be clear and exact in meaning _____

6. to put on as a duty, burden, or penalty _____

Chapter 4

Chapter 5 Elements of a Contract
Section 5.1 Capacity and Legality

 Note Taking

Directions As you read, write notes, facts, and main ideas in the Note Taking column. Write key words and short phrases in the Cues column. Then summarize the section in the Summary box.

Cues	Note Taking
• Minor: not yet reached age of majority (18 in most states)	**CAPACITY** • Capacity is the legal ability to enter a contract, deeming it valid. **LEGALITY** • Determines whether a contract is valid **STATUTE OF FRAUDS** • State law requires certain contracts be in writing so there is evidence that the contract exists and has definitive terms. • Examples: • Interpretation of written contracts must follow certain rules:

Summary

In order for contracts to be deemed valid, certain criteria must be met.

Chapter 5

Chapter 5 Elements of a Contract
Section 5.1 Capacity and Legality

Social Studies
Public Policy, Statutes, and Contracts

Directions Certain contracts violate either statutes or public policy. Match each statute or public policy below with the contract or agreement that violates it. Place the letter on the line next to the matching violation.

Statute or Public Policy

a. Civil and criminal statutes
b. Agreement involving price fixing
c. Usury statute
d. Agreement to give up the right to litigate or arbitrate
e. Gambling statute
f. Agreement that defeats competitive bidding
g. Sunday statute
h. Agreement interfering with marriage
i. Agreement to obstruct justice
j. Agreement inducing breach of duty or fraud

Contract or Agreement

_____ **1.** This contract involves one party attempting to collect a gambling debt from another.

_____ **2.** This contract involves a set of competitors agreeing to sell their product at a certain price.

_____ **3.** This agreement limits the ability of one party to bring a lawsuit against the other.

_____ **4.** This agreement requires one party to refrain from contacting family members.

_____ **5.** In this contract, an offer is made on Saturday and accepted on Sunday.

_____ **6.** This agreement requires one party to commit a tort or crime.

_____ **7.** This agreement involves a lender charging more than the maximum legal interest rate.

_____ **8.** This agreement involves a government official using his or her position for private gain.

_____ **9.** This agreement involves firms agreeing not to bid lower than a certain price on government projects.

_____ **10.** This agreement involves offering to pay a juror to find a defendant not guilty.

Chapter 5 Elements of a Contract
Section 5.1 Capacity and Legality

 Study Skills
Study Strategies

Directions Read the tips below. Then answer the questions that follow. Circle the letter of the answer that best completes each sentence.

STUDY STRATEGIES
• Use a desk calendar or student planner to record assignments as soon as you learn about them. Include the date the assignment is due. Block out enough time to do the work and complete the assignment on time. • Use a different color pen or marker for each class. • Record upcoming test dates. Mark these with a highlighter so they stand out. Block out extra study time to prepare for the test.

1. Capacity is the legal ability to
   a. disaffirm a contract.
   b. enter into a contract.
   c. assume that an argument is untrue.
   d. show intent not to live up to a contract.

2. The Statute of Frauds requires that certain contracts be
   a. fair to all parties involved.
   b. read by the court prior to signature.
   c. written so there is evidence that the contract exists and has definitive terms.
   d. free of stipulations.

3. To disaffirm a contract means to
   a. agree to all terms and conditions.
   b. prove a contract valid or invalid.
   c. renew an existing contract.
   d. show the intent not to live up to the contract.

4. An emancipated minor is one who
   a. is under the legal control of his or her parents.
   b. is no longer under the legal control of his or her parents.
   c. lacks the legal capacity to enter into a contract.
   d. shows intent not to live up to a contract.

5. Ratification is the act of agreeing to
   a. void a contract.
   b. search a minor student.
   c. go along with the terms of a contract that could have been voided.
   d. sue one of the parties to a contract.

Chapter 5 Elements of a Contract
Section 5.1 Capacity and Legality

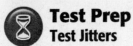
Test Prep
Test Jitters

Directions Read the tips below. Then answer the questions that follow.

TIPS FOR TEST JITTERS
• Having jitters before and during a test is normal, so do not worry about those butterflies in your stomach.
• Keep in mind that this is only one test. Each test is important, but it is not the only test on which your grade depends.
• When you feel nervous, take a deep breath. Clear your mind as you hold your breath. Exhale gently.
• Rest is important. Get plenty of sleep the night before a test.
• Dress in layers. If you get hot, you can remove one layer, or you can put one on if you get cold. Being comfortable during a test is important.

1. Who is required by law to determine if a person was mentally impaired upon entering into an agreement?

_____

_____

2. What is the definition of a minor?

_____

_____

3. What is the definition of an emancipated minor?

_____

_____

4. What is one way a minor can ratify a contract?

_____

_____

5. Under what circumstances may a student be searched by the authorities?

_____

_____

6. Explain one reason why certain states require people to have a license to do certain jobs.

_____

_____

Chapter 5 Elements of a Contract
Section 5.2 Consideration

 Note Taking

Directions As you read, write notes, facts, and main ideas in the Note Taking column. Write key words and short phrases in the Cues column. Then summarize the section in the Summary box.

Cues	Note Taking
• Benefits and detriments are decided by all parties involved.	**CONSIDERATION** • Consideration: exchange of benefits and detriments by the parties to a contract • Three types of detriment: **TYPES OF CONSIDERATION** • Money **PROBLEMS WITH CONSIDERATION** • When amount owed is disputed, parties can use accord and satisfaction to settle. • Some agreements are valid w/o consideration: • Promises under seal

Summary
Consideration is the exchange of benefits and detriments by the parties to a contract.

Chapter 5 Elements of a Contract
Section 5.2 Consideration

 Mathematics
Using a Chart

Directions Review the column "Agreement Between Parties" in the chart below. In the first column, fill in which type of consideration is involved. Next, determine whether each agreement is a legal contract. Explain your answers. The first one has been done for you.

Type of Consideration	Agreement Between Parties	Legal Contract?
Money	George takes out a loan from the bank and agrees to pay the amount, plus interest, back to the bank.	Yes. It involves the exchange of money in return for the promise to pay it back.
	A neighborhood boy takes it upon himself to shovel the driveways of his neighbors after a snowstorm. He then asks his neighbors for payment in return for his service.	
	Scott purchases stolen property by writing a check.	
	After assessing the damage to a local bar after a fight, the prosecutor agrees not to press charges against those guilty if they agree to pay for the repairs.	
	Edward donated $1,000 to a local charity knowing that he would receive no direct benefit in return.	

Chapter 5 Elements of a Contract
Section 5.2 Consideration

Study Skills
Practicing Good Study Habits

Directions Read the tips below. Then answer the questions that follow by writing a check mark (✓) for each "yes" answer. If you cannot answer "yes" to each question, you may need to improve your study habits.

TIPS FOR GOOD STUDY HABITS
• Review class material every day instead of "cramming" it all in just before a test.
• Be alert in class and take good notes.
• Complete all assignments given by your instructor.
• Study with classmates to learn from their points of view.
• Maintain an organized notebook and folder for each separate subject.
• Ask your instructor if you do not understand certain material.
• Keep the television or radio off while studying.
• Get plenty of sleep each night so you can better concentrate on your studies.

Question	Yes!
Have I studied today's class material?	✓
Am I paying attention in class and taking good notes?	
Have I completed today's homework assignment?	
Which classmates will I benefit from studying with or be able to help?	
Do I have an organized notebook or folder for each of my classes?	
Have I asked my instructor about any material I do not understand?	
Am I studying without the television or radio?	
Am I getting enough sleep each night?	

How can I improve my study habits to maximize my learning potential?

_____

_____

_____

_____

Chapter 5

Chapter 5 Elements of a Contract
Section 5.2 Consideration

Test Taking
What to Do During a Test

Directions Read the tips below. Then answer the questions that follow by writing the correct answers in the space provided.

TEST-TAKING TIPS
• Read the test directions carefully. Underline words that will help you follow directions, such as *summarize, compare and contrast*, or *explain your answer*. • When you have finished the test, check your answers to make sure you have answered every question. • For essay and short-answer questions, reread your answers. Check spelling, grammar, and sentence structure.

1. Which is one of the three characteristics of consideration?
   a. The benefits and detriments that make up consideration must be legal.
   b. doing what you have the right not to do
   c. refusing to enforce the entire contract
   d. marking a contract to indicate that it is a formal agreement

   _____

2. Which of the following is not a type of consideration?
   a. money   **c.** writing a fair contract
   b. property   **d.** a promise not to sue

   _____

3. Which of the following is not a type of detriment?
   a. giving up something that you have the right to keep
   b. reading the terms of the agreement
   c. doing something that you have the right not to do
   d. not doing something that you have the legal right to do

   _____

4. Which is a contractual situation in which consideration does not apply?
   a. an exchange of money for goods or services **c.** an exchange of money for property
   b. a charitable pledge   **d.** a promise not to sue

   _____

5. What does the term *forbearance* mean?
   a. giving up something that you have the right to keep
   b. exchanging something of value for something else of value
   c. not doing what you have the legal right to do
   d. offering a service as consideration

   _____

Chapter 5 Elements of a Contract
Chapter Content Vocabulary

English Language Arts
Reading Skills

Directions For each term or phrase, write one or two sentences to show that you understand its meaning. The first one has been done for you.

1. disaffirm The agreement did not protect his interests, therefore Joe decided to disaffirm the
contract and make it void.

2. majority _____

_____

3. capacity _____

_____

4. forbearance _____

_____

5. consideration _____

_____

6. minor _____

_____

7. public policy _____

_____

8. ratification _____

_____

9. unconscionable contract _____

_____

10. adhesion contract _____

_____

Chapter 5

Chapter 5 Elements of a Contract
Chapter Academic Vocabulary
 English Language Arts
Vocabulary

Directions Fill in the bubble of the phrase that best completes each sentence.

1. **Usury** is an example of an activity that
   ○ has the potential to provide both parties with cash benefits.
   ○ has the hidden dimension of illegality.
   ○ assures fair treatment to all parties to an agreement.
   ○ is exercised by the court.

2. A contract that gets in the way of the **dispensing** of justice is
   ○ standard procedure.
   ○ a legal way to conduct business.
   ○ illegal.
   ○ rare.

3. The **assumption** that a person has the capacity to enter into a contract is called
   ○ rebuttable presumption.
   ○ ratification.
   ○ age of majority.
   ○ the parol evidence rule.

4. The agreed-upon settlement as **contained** in the accord
   ○ is an illusory promise.
   ○ can be declared void by either party.
   ○ is the satisfaction.
   ○ is unenforceable.

5. A seal is a mark or an impression placed on a written contract **indicating**
   ○ that the contract is old.
   ○ how many parties are involved.
   ○ that the terms favor one party over the other.
   ○ that it is a formal agreement.

6. A preexisting duty is an **obligation** that
   ○ a person can use again in a new contract.
   ○ benefits both parties.
   ○ already commits a person to do something.
   ○ takes advantage of the other parties involved.

Chapter 5

Chapter 6 How Contracts Come to an End
Section 6.1 Transferring and Ending Contracts

 Note Taking

Directions As you read, write notes, facts, and main ideas in the Note Taking column. Write key words and short phrases in the Cues column. Then summarize the section in the Summary box.

Cues	Note Taking
• Discharged: when a contract comes to an end	**ENDING A CONTRACT** • Contracts may be ended by performance or by agreement. **DISCHARGE BY PERFORMANCE** • Performance is a series of activities that fulfill a contract. **DISCHARGE BY AGREEMENT** • Can be by mutual release or by accord and satisfaction **DISCHARGE BY IMPOSSIBILITY OF PERFORMANCE** • Three situations can prevent performance of a contract: **DISCHARGE BY OPERATION OF LAW** • Contracts may end in the best interest of society. **TRANSFER OF RIGHTS AND DUTIES** • Contract rights can be transferred as long as contract does not say they cannot.

Summary
Contracts may be discharged if the duties have been fulfilled or if the agreement has been broken.

Chapter 6 How Contracts Come to an End

Section 6.1 Transferring and Ending Contracts

 Social Studies
Ending Contracts

Directions Study the list below of ways to end contracts. Match each with one of the examples of discharged contracts that follow. Write the letter next to the matching example. Not all terms will be used.

WAYS TO END CONTRACTS

a. satisfactory performance
b. substantial performance
c. tender of performance
d. mutual release
e. accord and satisfaction
f. impossibility of performance
g. wrongful alteration
h. statute of limitations

EXAMPLES OF DISCHARGED CONTRACTS

_____ **1.** A contractor agreed to use a certain type of sealer specified by the owner to resurface a driveway. When the contractor performed the work, he used a different sealer. The owner sued to be discharged from the contract.

_____ **2.** A builder agreed to construct an addition onto an existing home. The builder completed the project satisfactorily but forgot to install a porch light. The owner of the home refused to pay the builder for any work done. The builder offered to deduct the amount for installing the porch light from his final bill. The owner agreed.

_____ **3.** A person signed up for ten dance lessons and paid the dance instructor in advance. The dance instructor injured her ankle and was not able to provide the lessons. She refunded the person's money.

_____ **4.** A contractor installed replacement windows in a home. The homeowner was unhappy with the molding around the new windows and refused to pay for the work. The contractor offered to replace the molding with one satisfactory to the homeowner. The homeowner refused the offer and paid only part of the total amount owed. A court ordered the homeowner to pay the full amount.

_____ **5.** An artist agreed to create a painting for a buyer for $1,000. Upon completion of the painting, the artist sent it to the buyer. The buyer received it and asked the artist when the frame would be delivered. The artist was not aware that the price included a frame. The buyer was so happy with the painting, however, that she agreed to accept it without a frame.

Chapter 6 How Contracts Come to an End
Section 6.1 Transferring and Ending Contracts

 **Study Skills**
Memorizing

Directions Read the tips below. Then answer the questions that follow.

TECHNIQUES FOR MEMORIZING
• Make a link. Associate an unfamiliar idea or word with something you already know.   • Make an acronym. Create a word or words using the first letter of each word you want to remember.   • Be creative. Think of a catchy saying related to the idea or word that creates a mental picture of it in your mind.   • Be humorous. Take the first letter of each word or phrase you want to remember. Create words from the letters and put them together into funny phrases or sentences.   • Make a rhyme or song. Set long lists of facts to a rhyme or to the tune of a familiar song.

1. What memory technique could you use to remember the difference between satisfactory performance and substantial performance?

_____

_____

_____

2. What memory technique could you use to understand the concept of tender of performance?

_____

_____

_____

3. What memory technique could you use to remember the three situations of impossibility of performance?

_____

_____

_____

4. What memory technique could you use to list all the ways a contract can be discharged?

_____

_____

_____

Chapter 6

Chapter 6 How Contracts Come to an End
Section 6.1 Transferring and Ending Contracts

 Test Taking
Short-Answer Questions

Directions Read the tips below. Then answer the practice test questions that follow.

TIPS FOR SHORT-ANSWER TESTS
• Reread the question several times.   • Look for context clues in the question.   • Check the verb in the question. If it is singular, the answer must be singular. If it is plural, the answer must be plural.

1. A series of activities that fulfill the purpose of a contract is called _____.

2. _____ is determined by what is suitable, fair, and proper to the goal of the contract.

3. _____ is a situation in which a party has, in good faith, completed the major requirements of a contract, leaving only a few minor details unfinished.

4. Accord and satisfaction occurs when one party agrees to _____ one contract for another.

5. The two primary ways contracts are discharged involuntarily are by impossibility of performance and by _____.

6. _____ means that people can create contracts by mutual agreement, and they can end contracts the same way.

7. If the means or subject matter that is needed to perform the contract is destroyed through no fault of either party, the contract is _____.

8. A _____ establishes a time limit for suing in a civil case, based on the date when the breach occurred or was discovered.

Chapter 6 How Contracts Come to an End
Section 6.2 Voidable Contracts and Remedies

 Note Taking

Directions As you read, write notes, facts, and main ideas in the Note Taking column. Write key words and short phrases in the Cues column. Then summarize the section in the Summary box.

Cues	Note Taking
• Remedy: legal means of enforcing a right or correcting a wrong	**DEFECTIVE AGREEMENTS** • Several circumstances might lead to a defective agreement. • Five elements must be shown to prove fraud: • Duress: destroying somebody's free will by force, threat of force, or bodily harm • Undue influence: inappropriate use of one person's power over another to create a favorable agreement to the more powerful person **REMEDIES AND DAMAGES** • Money damages should put you in the position you would have been in had the contract been carried out.

Summary
There are several ways that a contract may be breached: fraud, mistake, duress, and undue influence.

Chapter 6 How Contracts Come to an End
Section 6.2 Voidable Contracts and Remedies

 English Language Arts
Writing

Directions Read the tips below. Then write one or two paragraphs on the remedies available to a person whose contract has been breached.

TIPS FOR WRITING GOOD PARAGRAPHS
• A paragraph should contain a topic sentence that provides the main idea of the paragraph. The topic sentence is often the first sentence in the paragraph.
• The remaining sentences should provide details to support and clarify the main idea of the paragraph.
• Vary the length of the sentences to make the paragraph more interesting and easier to read.
• Get rid of unnecessary words that might distract the reader from the main idea.

_____

_____

_____

_____

_____

_____

_____

_____

_____

_____

_____

_____

_____

_____

_____

_____

_____

_____

_____

_____

_____

Chapter 6 How Contracts Come to an End
Section 6.2 Voidable Contracts and Remedies

Study Skills
Learning Styles

Directions Read the information in the box below. Then answer the questions that follow.

KNOW YOUR LEARNING STYLES
People learn in different ways. It is important to know which ways are easier or harder for you. Once you determine them, you will know your strengths and weaknesses. Capitalize on your strengths and work on improving your weaknesses.

- Auditory learners: people who learn best by listening, such as to a teacher's lecture
- Visual learners: people who learn best by seeing, such as reading or viewing a demonstration
- Tactile learners: people who learn best by touching or doing, such as writing or performing an action

1. If you are a tactile learner, how could you become better organized?

_____

_____

2. If you are an auditory learner, how could you better prepare for a test?

_____

_____

3. If you are a visual learner, how could you remember what you hear while listening to a class lecture?

_____

_____

4. If you are a tactile learner, how could you remember what you hear while listening to a class lecture?

_____

_____

5. If you are a visual learner, how could you remember what you hear while listening to a class lecture?

_____

_____

Chapter 6 How Contracts Come to an End
Section 6.2 Voidable Contracts and Remedies

 Test Prep
Open-Book Tests

Directions Read the tips below. Then answer the questions that follow.

PREPARING FOR AN OPEN-BOOK TEST

- Stay up-to-date by reading the text and reviewing your notes every day. You may use both the text and your notes in an open-book test.
- Use sticky notes in the margins of your text to mark important points to remember. Write key words on the sticky notes.
- Use different color highlighters to mark your notes. For example, use orange for important dates, yellow for key words and definitions, pink for major ideas. When you scan your notes, you can identify the information quickly by color.
- Organize and edit the notes that you want to take with you to the test. Do not overburden yourself with too many notes. Remember, time is limited on the test, so get organized! Make sure you can find everything you need quickly.

---

1. What materials can you use in an open-book test?

   _____

   _____

2. How can you use sticky notes to help you?

   _____

   _____

3. How will it help to highlight your notes in different colors?

   _____

   _____

4. Why is organization important prior to the test?

   _____

   _____

5. Would you say that an open-book test is easier or harder than a closed-book test? Explain your answer.

   _____

   _____

Chapter 6 How Contracts Come to an End
Chapter Content Vocabulary

English Language Arts
Writing

Directions Use at least eight of the words below in a short essay. The essay should show that you understand the meaning of each word.

substantial performance	fraud
tender	duress
discharge by agreement	undue influence
impossibility of performance	remedy
statute of limitations	damages
assignment	punitive damages
delegation	injunction
breach of contract	

_____

_____

_____

_____

_____

_____

_____

_____

_____

_____

_____

_____

_____

_____

_____

_____

_____

Chapter 6

Chapter 6 How Contracts Come to an End
Chapter Academic Vocabulary

 English Language Arts
Reading Skills

Directions Use the words in the box below to complete each sentence that follows. Write the word on the line provided.

substituted	intent
expire	exaggerate
affected	mutual

1. One contract that is replaced by another is said to be _____.

2. Debts for taxes, alimony, child support, and maintenance are not _____ by a general discharge of debts of bankruptcy.

3. When the obligations of a contract end despite what the parties intended, the contract may also _____.

4. The law allows sellers to _____ their claims as long as the claims are obviously a statement of the seller's opinion.

5. A bilateral mistake, also called a(n) _____ mistake, is an error made by both parties to a contract.

6. For fraud, a lie must be made with the _____ that it will be relied on.

Chapter 7 Consumer Law and Contracts

Section 7.1 Sales Contracts

 Note Taking

Directions As you read, write notes, facts, and main ideas in the Note Taking column. Write key words and short phrases in the Cues column. Then summarize the section in the Summary box.

Cues	Note Taking
• UCC: collection of laws that governs various types of business transactions	**SALES OF GOODS** • Sales law governs the sale of goods. • Uniform Commercial Code (UCC) was enacted to make sales law uniform among states. **SPECIAL RULES** • Special rules apply to contracts for the sale of goods: **TITLE AND RISK OF LOSS** • People who own goods have title to them. **BREACH OF SALES CONTRACT** • Buyers and sellers can seek remedies when a contract is breached.

Summary
A sales contract is bound by law but may be breached by the buyer or seller.

Chapter 7

Chapter 7 Consumer Law and Contracts
Section 7.1 Sales Contracts

 Reading Comprehension
Reading a Table

Directions Study the table below. Use the facts to answer the questions that follow.

Buyers' Remedies	Sellers' Remedies
Cancel contract.	Cancel contract.
Bring a claim against seller for the return of money paid.	Withhold delivery of goods.
Bring a claim against seller for the difference between agreed price and market price.	Stop delivery of any goods held by a carrier.
Refuse to accept goods if something is wrong with them. Give seller time to correct problem.	Bring a claim against buyer for the price of any goods that buyer accepted.
Buy similar goods from someone else and bring a claim against seller for the difference between agreed price and cost of purchase.	Resell any goods that have been rightfully withheld, and bring a claim against buyer for the difference between agreed price and resale price.
Give notice to seller that the goods have been accepted but something is wrong with them. If no adjustment is made, buyer may bring a claim against seller for breach of contract.	If goods cannot be resold, bring a claim against buyer for the difference between agreed upon price and market price.
Revoke acceptance and return goods if a serious defect was undetectable, or if buyer was led to believe seller would fix defect.	

1. What remedy applies to both buyer and seller when a sales contract has been breached?

_____

_____

2. If you buy new office furniture and notice it is damaged when it is delivered, what options do you have?

_____

_____

3. If a buyer breaches a sales contract, must the seller still deliver the goods?

_____

_____

Chapter 7 Consumer Law and Contracts
Section 7.1 Sales Contracts

 Study Skills
Improving Learning Skills

Directions Read the tips below. Then answer the questions that follow.

IMPROVING LEARNING SKILLS
• Summarize a section after you read it.
• Ask yourself questions about the subject you are studying.
• Use different sources to obtain information about the subject.
• Use different methods to learn information. For example, read the text aloud. This stimulates more areas of your brain. You are learning both visually and auditorily.
• Find the conditions that are best for you. For example, join a study group, or find a quiet place if you study best alone.
• Think about other things you have learned and how you learned them. Did you learn by reading, having someone show you, looking at pictures and graphs, or listening to someone speak? Use these same ways of learning when studying new material.

1. Name something you have learned to do. Explain how you learned to do it.

   _____

   _____

2. How might understanding how you learn help you improve your learning skills?

   _____

   _____

3. How might summarizing a section after reading it help you learn?

   _____

   _____

4. How might asking questions help you learn?

   _____

5. Why is it important to use different sources to learn? Name three sources you might use.

   _____

   _____

6. How might using different methods of learning at the same time help you learn?

   _____

   _____

Chapter 7 Consumer Law and Contracts

Section 7.1 Sales Contracts

Test Taking
Test-Taking Strategies

Directions Read the tips below. Then answer the questions that follow.

TEST-TAKING TIPS
• Read all instructions carefully before you begin.
• Make sure you understand the directions. Ask the teacher if you do not understand some of the directions.
• Read the entire test before you start, so you know what types of questions are on the test.
• Take note of the point value of each question or section. This will help you pace yourself.
• Answer the easiest questions first. Then answer the questions with the highest point value.

1. Why should you ask your teacher if you do not understand some of the directions?

_____

_____

2. Why should you read the whole test before you start?

_____

_____

3. Why do you need to pay attention to the point value of each section?

_____

_____

4. Why should you answer the easiest questions first?

_____

_____

5. Why should you answer the questions with the highest point values before answering those with lower point values?

_____

_____

Chapter 7 Consumer Law and Contracts
Section 7.2 Consumer Protection

 Note Taking

Directions As you read, write notes, facts, and main ideas in the Note Taking column. Write key words and short phrases in the Cues column. Then summarize the section in the Summary box.

Cues	Note Taking
• Consumer buys or leases goods, real estate, or services for personal, family, or household purposes. • FTC promotes free and fair trade competition.	**CONSUMER PROTECTION LAWS** • Federal and state governments have laws to protect the well-being of consumers. • Unfair and deceptive practices: • Federal Trade Commission rules: **WARRANTIES** • A warranty is a guarantee that a product will perform as promised. • Types of express warranties: • Types of implied warranties:

Summary
Agencies, laws, and warranties all help protect consumers.

Chapter 7

Chapter 7 Consumer Law and Contracts
Section 7.2 Consumer Protection

English Language Arts
Proofreading

Directions Read the tips below. In each of the two paragraphs that follow, correct the errors using proofreader's marks. Then rewrite the corrected paragraph on the lines provided.

PROOFREADING TIPS
• Check for capitalization in the first word of a sentence and in all proper nouns. Put three lines under a letter that needs to be capitalized: june.
• Check for correct punctuation at the end of a sentence. Be sure that periods, question marks, and exclamation points are used correctly.
• Make sure commas are used to separate items in a series: red, white, and blue.
• Use a caret to insert missing text: Laws protect consumers.
• Use a delete mark to take out extra text: deelete.
• Check spelling. Start at the end of the text and work backward through the copy. Check one word at a time.

State consumer protektion laws are designed to protect consumers from deceptive and unfair practices? Laws like these exist in almost every states, although the details vary. read about a consumer who has been helped by such laws.

In ohio, a car dealer promised a "free three-day, two-night vacation to Las Vegas" to anyone who bought a car or van. Based on this special prommotion, Jack bought a car from the dealer. When the vacation voucher came in the mail, Jack discovered that the trip had many restrictions conditions and obligations he was not informed of. Thinking she had been ripped off, Jack sued the car dealer. The jury awarded Jac $1,852 in compensatory damages (the value of the vacation), plus $6,000 in punitive damages.

_____

_____

_____

_____

_____

_____

_____

_____

Chapter 7 Consumer Law and Contracts
Section 7.2 Consumer Protection

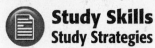 **Study Skills**
Study Strategies

Directions Read the tips below. Then answer the questions that follow by circling the letter of the word or phrase that best completes each sentence.

TIPS FOR STUDY STRATEGIES
• Use a monthly calendar or student planner to record class assignments as soon as you learn about them. Include the date the assignment is due. Block out study time so you can complete the assignment on time.
• Use a different color pen or highlighter for each class.
• Record upcoming test dates. Highlight these dates so they stand out. Block out extra study time.

1. A fraudulent misrepresentation is any statement that
   a. describes a buyer.
   b. cancels a contract.
   c. deceives a buyer.
   d. advertises a product.

2. The negative option rule applies to products that are sent
   a. by mistake.
   b. randomly.
   c. on a regular basis.
   d. to a business.

3. The cooling-off rule gives you three business days to
   a. extend a written sales contract to a buyer.
   b. cancel a transaction made away from a seller's regular place of business.
   c. refuse to promise delivery of the advertised product within a reasonable time.
   d. disclose something that is important to the consumer.

4. A warranty in the form of an actual sample of a product would be
   a. an express warranty.
   b. a warranty of fitness.
   c. a limited warranty.
   d. a warranty of title.

5. An implied warranty is a guarantee imposed by
   a. law.
   b. the manufacturer.
   c. the seller.
   d. the buyer.

Chapter 7 Consumer Law and Contracts
Section 7.2 Consumer Protection

Test Prep
Using a Checklist

Directions Read the tips below to help you fill in the checklist. Then use what you have learned to take the practice test that follows.

CHECKLIST TIPS
• Leave an inch in the left-hand border on the paper you will use for your checklist.
• Gather all the materials you will need, including your textbook and old tests.
• Gather all your notes, including your notes from reading the text and notes you took in class.
• Identify all the text material that you will need to know.
• Ask your teacher what else you need to know.
• Use your materials and notes to prepare. Turn headings into questions and answer those questions. Answer end-of-section questions. Answer any other questions in the text and in the margins.

Completed	Task
✓	Gather all materials and notes: • textbook • old tests • notes I took from the text • notes I took in class
	Identify all material I need to know. Ask my teacher what else I need to know.
	Turn headings into questions and answer them. Answer end-of-section questions. Answer questions in text and margins.

1. How would you define *consumer*?

   _____

   _____

2. What have individual states done to help protect consumers?

   _____

   _____

3. Name three FTC trade regulation rules.

   _____

   _____

Chapter 7 Consumer Law and Contracts
Chapter Content Vocabulary

English Language Arts
Writing

Directions Choose ten terms from the list below. Use each in a sentence that shows you understand the definition of the word.

Uniform Commercial Code (UCC)	insurable interest	full warranty
firm offer	voidable title	limited warranty
title	risk of loss	implied warranty
bill of sale	express warranty	warranty of merchantability
warranty		

1. _____

_____

2. _____

_____

3. _____

_____

4. _____

_____

5. _____

_____

6. _____

_____

7. _____

_____

8. _____

_____

9. _____

_____

10. _____

_____

Chapter 7

Chapter 7 Consumer Law and Contracts
Chapter Academic Vocabulary

 English Language Arts
Reading Skills

Directions Fill in the blank with the correct vocabulary word.

uniform	disclose
dominant	option
revoke	exclude

1. The _____ element determines the law that will apply when a contract includes goods and services.

2. When a seller does not _____ something important to the consumer, a fraudulent misrepresentation occurs.

3. The negative _____ rule applies when you subscribe to a magazine.

4. The UCC helps to make laws related to the sale of goods _____ among the states.

5. The word *merchantability* must be specifically mentioned in order to _____ the warranty of merchantability.

6. A merchant cannot _____ a firm offer during the time stated in the offer.

Chapter 8 Personal Property

Section 8.1 Types of Property

 Note Taking

Directions As you read, write notes, facts, and main ideas in the Note Taking
column. Write key words and short phrases in the Cues column. Then summarize
the section in the Summary box.

Cues	Note Taking
• Examples of fixtures: built-in stoves, cabinets • Examples of intellectual property:	**PERSONAL PROPERTY** • Personal property: everything that can be owned other than real property • Co-ownership of personal property: • Lost, misplaced, and stolen property • Three requirements of a completed gift: **INTELLECTUAL PROPERTY** • Intellectual property: original work fixed in a tangible medium of expression
Summary	
Personal property is anything, other than real property, that can be owned.	

Chapter 8 Personal Property

Section 8.1 Types of Property

 Social Studies
Making Inferences

Directions The chart below compares property inheritance rights of women in the United States to those of women in Kenya. Complete the chart based on your reading of the text. Then write one or two paragraphs about the role of women in Kenya.

WOMEN'S PROPERTY RIGHTS

United States	Kenya
Granted same rights in property as males	
Outlaws discrimination based on sex	
	Both male and female inherit equally if no surviving spouse. However, if surviving spouse is a woman and remarries, she loses all interest in the property.
Laws apply to members of all ethnic groups.	

_____

_____

_____

_____

_____

_____

Chapter 8

Chapter 8 Personal Property
Section 8.1 Types of Property

Study Skills
Monitoring Comprehension

Directions Read the tips below. Then answer the questions that follow.

MONITORING COMPREHENSION
While you read your text, it is important to stop occasionally to monitor how well you understand what you are reading. When you stop, ask yourself these questions: • Can I put the main ideas into my own words?   • Do I need to look up any words to be sure of their meaning?   • Do I understand how the new information fits in with information I have already learned?   • Do I need to read any sections over again?   • Can I predict what will happen next?

1. In your own words, summarize the main ideas of Section 8.1 in the text.

_____

_____

_____

2. What words in Section 8.1 do you not know the meaning of? List them and use a dictionary to write a definition for each one.

_____

_____

_____

3. How are laws governing property similar to the consumer laws you read about in Chapter 7?

_____

_____

_____

4. Section 8.2 of the text is titled Bailments. Although you may not know what this word means, what do you think it relates to?

_____

_____

_____

Chapter 8

Chapter 8 Personal Property
Section 8.1 Types of Property

Test Taking
Using Flash Cards

Directions Study the instructions below on making flash cards. Complete the chart that follows by organizing the information you learned in Section 8.1 into questions and answers. Then make a set of flash cards by following the instructions.

FLASH CARD TIPS
• Use 3" by 5" index cards for your flash cards.
• Create questions and answers from headings, key words, end-of-section questions, end-of-chapter questions, and any questions in the text or margins.
• Write a question on the front side of an index card. On the back, write the answer. Repeat with the remaining index cards.
• Mix up the flash cards. Look at the front of the first card. Read the question aloud. Then answer the question.
• Turn the card over to check your answer.

Front Side	Back Side
What is personal property?	Everything, other than real property, that can be owned

Chapter 8 Personal Property
Section 8.2 Bailments

 Note Taking

Directions As you read, write notes, facts, and main ideas in the Note Taking column. Write key words and short phrases in the Cues column. Then summarize the section in the Summary box.

Cues	Note Taking
• Bailor transfers property.	**BAILMENTS** • Bailment: transfer of possession of personal property to another with the intent that the property will be returned later • Standard of care (special bailment): bailee liable for damage

Summary
A bailment is the transfer of possession and control of personal property to another with the intent that the property be returned later.

Chapter 8

Chapter 8 Personal Property
Section 8.2 Bailments

Reading Skills
Drawing Conclusions

Directions Read the tips below on improving your reading comprehension by drawing conclusions. Then, for each situation that follows, draw a conclusion about who is responsible. Explain your answers in the space provided.

DRAWING CONCLUSIONS
When you draw a conclusion, think about the facts that you have read. Then reach a decision, or conclusion, that makes sense based on those facts. After you draw a conclusion, ask yourself these questions: • Does my conclusion make sense? • Could someone else draw a different conclusion? • Do I have enough facts to draw a conclusion? • Are the facts accurate?

Situation	Person Responsible
A friend asks you to watch his camera while he uses a public restroom. He places the camera on the table in front of you. While you are waiting, another person bumps the table. The camera falls to the ground, breaking the lens. Are you liable for the damage?	
You drop off your car at a garage to be repaired. The mechanic gives you an estimate for the repairs. You agree to have him perform the work. The mechanic stacks some tools next to your car. The tools fall and hit your car, making a large dent. Is the mechanic liable for the damage?	
You are in possession of an antique table that you wish to sell. You consign the antique to a dealer who will try to sell it for you. The dealer arrives at the gallery one morning and notices a large scratch on the table. The dealer never noticed the scratch before and does not know how it got there. Who is responsible for the damage?	
You check into a hotel room and leave to eat at a nearby restaurant. While you are gone, another hotel guest accidentally sets the building on fire by leaving an iron turned on. Your possessions are destroyed in the fire. Is the hotel keeper liable for your property loss?	

Chapter 8

Chapter 8 Personal Property

Section 8.2 Bailments

Study Skills
Recording Information

Directions Read the information in the box below. Then, in groups of three or four, discuss what bailments have taken place in the last week for each of you. Write the different bailments and the type of bailments in the topic web that follows.

USING TOPIC WEBS
Topic webs are a good way to organize information around related topics. Start by writing a topic in the center oval below. In this case, the topic is bailments. Then, in the outer ovals, write ideas or facts related to the topic to complete the web. Repeat the procedure with your own topic webs. Use the topic webs to study and memorize related information or write a paragraph about it.

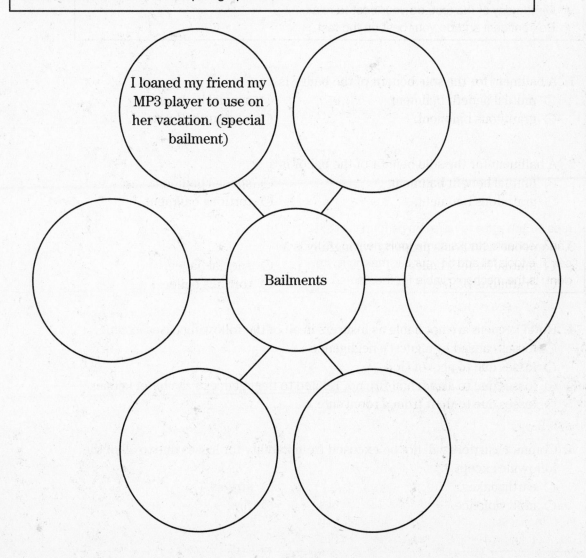

Chapter 8 Personal Property

Section 8.2 Bailments

 Test Prep
Preparing for a Test

Directions Read the tips below. Then take the practice test that follows by filling in the bubble next to the correct answer.

TEST PREPARATION TIPS
• Organize the notes you took while reading the text and the notes you took while in class. • Set aside time you will need to study for the test. • Test yourself on the material. • Finish studying the day before the exam. Write down specific information that is hard for you to grasp. Review it right before you go to bed the night before the test. • Get a good night's sleep. • On the day of the test, do your best to relax. • Be confident and do your best on the test.

1. A bailment for the sole benefit of the bailee is a
- ○ mutual benefit bailment.
- ○ gratuitous bailment.
- ○ special bailment.
- ○ tortious bailment.

2. A bailment for the sole benefit of the bailor is a
- ○ mutual benefit bailment.
- ○ gratuitous bailment.
- ○ special bailment.
- ○ tortious bailment.

3. Someone who holds property wrongfully is a
- ○ mutual benefit bailee.
- ○ gratuitous bailee.
- ○ special bailee.
- ○ tortious bailee.

4. Hotel keepers are not liable as insurers in all of the following cases except
- ○ losses caused by a guest's negligence.
- ○ losses due to acts of God.
- ○ losses due to accidental fire not related to negligence of the hotel keeper.
- ○ losses due to theft from a room safe.

5. Common carriers will not be excused from liability for losses due to all of the following except
- ○ earthquakes.
- ○ mob violence.
- ○ strikes.
- ○ fire.

Chapter 8 Personal Property

Chapter Content Vocabulary

 English Language Arts
Writing

Directions Fill in the blanks with the correct vocabulary term.

bailment	carrier
common carrier	copyright
gratuitous bailment	intellectual property
mutual benefit bailment	patent
personal property	special bailment
trademark	

1. A(n) _____ is a bailment in which both parties receive some benefit.

2. A(n) _____ is a right granted to an author, composer, photographer, or artist to exclusively publish and sell a work.

3. _____ is everything except real property that can be owned.

4. A(n) _____ is a bailment for the sole benefit of the bailor.

5. A(n) _____ is a grant giving an inventor the exclusive right to an invention for a set period of time.

6. _____ is an original work fixed in a tangible medium of expression.

7. A(n) _____ is the transfer of possession and control of personal property to another with the intent that the same property will be returned later.

8. A(n) _____ is a business that transports persons, goods, or both.

9. A(n) _____ is compensated for providing transportation to the general public.

10. A(n) _____ is a bailment for the sole benefit of the bailee.

11. A distinctive mark, symbol, or slogan used to identify and distinguish a business's goods is called a(n) _____.

Chapter 8

Chapter 8 Personal Property
Chapter Academic Vocabulary

 English Language Arts
Reading Skills

Directions Match each word below to its definition. Write the letter of the word on the line next to its definition.

a. tangible
b. exclusive
c. downloading
d. standard
e. benefit
f. register

1. _____ a help or advantage

2. _____ given or belonging to no other

3. _____ to put one's name in a record

4. _____ to obtain information from someone else's computer through a network

5. _____ something of substance that can be touched

6. _____ a rule or model with which other things like it are compared

Chapter 9 Renting or Owning a Home
Section 9.1 Rental Agreements

 Note Taking

Directions As you read, write notes, facts, and main ideas in the Note Taking column. Write key words and short phrases in the Cues column. Then summarize the section in the Summary box.

Cues	Note Taking
• Tenant: rents real property	**LANDLORD-TENANT RELATIONSHIP** • A lease states that the tenant is the lessee and the landlord is the lessor. • Types of tenancy: **LANDLORD-TENANT RESPONSIBILITIES** • Both landlord and tenant have legal obligations. • Landlord's obligations: • Tenant's obligations: **EVICTION** • Eviction occurs when landlord deprives tenant of possession of premises for neglecting the terms of the lease.

Summary

A lease creates the landlord-tenant relationship.

Name _____ Date _____ Class _____

Chapter 9 Renting or Owning a Home
Section 9.1 Rental Agreements

 Reading Skills
Using a Table

Directions Both landlord and tenant have responsibilities that are outlined in a lease. Read the list of responsibilities in the first column. Decide which belongs to the landlord and which to the tenant. Place a check mark in the corresponding column.

Responsibility	Landlord	Tenant
To refrain from discrimination based on race, religion, color, gender, age, or marital status		
To return built-in stoves, kitchen cabinets, and light fixtures upon vacating premises		
To transfer exclusive peaceful possession and quiet enjoyment of the premises		
To avoid damaging or destroying the property		
To offer property that is clean, properly heated, furnished with utilities, and safe		

Chapter 9

Chapter 9 Renting or Owning a Home
Section 9.1 Rental Agreements

Study Skills
Critical Thinking

Directions Read the tips below. Then answer the questions that follow.

CRITICAL-THINKING TIPS
Thinking critically is important when taking in new material and information. Ask yourself these questions to improve your critical-thinking skills when reading or listening. • Am I being objective and honest when I think about and react to what I am reading or listening to? • Am I thinking things through completely before taking a stance on what I believe? • Am I looking for evidence on which to base my decisions? • Do I ask myself questions while reading or listening to new information? • Do I refrain from being manipulated by what I hear or read?

1. Most landlords require a security deposit from a tenant. The deposit is held until completion of the lease and returned to the tenant if no damage has occurred to the property. Do you think this is fair to both tenant and landlord? Explain your answer.

   _____

   _____

2. Why is it important to have a formal lease agreement in writing?

   _____

   _____

3. A landlord has stipulated in a lease that the tenant will be responsible for the financial costs of repairing any excessive waste or damage to the property. Do you think this is fair to both tenant and landlord? Explain your answer.

   _____

   _____

4. You have told your landlord of maintenance problems, and the landlord has not responded. In some states, it is legal for you to correct the problems at your own expense and deduct the amount from the rent. Do you think this is fair? Explain your answer.

   _____

   _____

   _____

Chapter 9

Chapter 9 Renting or Owning a Home
Section 9.1 Rental Agreements

Test Taking
Using a Checklist

Directions Read the tips below to help you fill in the checklist. Then use what you have learned to take the practice test that follows.

CHECKLIST TIPS
• Leave an inch in the left-hand border on the paper you will use for your checklist. This space will be for the check marks.
• Gather all the materials you will need, including your textbook and old tests.
• Gather all your notes, including your notes from reading the text and notes you took in class.
• Identify all the text material that you will need to know.
• Ask your teacher what else you need to know.
• Use your materials and notes to prepare. Turn headings into questions and answer those questions. Answer end-of-section questions. Answer any other questions in the text and in the margins.

Completed	Task
✓	Gather all materials and notes: • textbook • notes I took from the text • old tests • notes I took in class
	Identify all material I need to know. Ask my teacher what else I need to know.
	Turn headings into questions and answer them. Answer end-of-section questions. Answer questions in text and margins.

1. Why is it important for a landlord to stipulate that all permanent fixtures be turned over to the landlord at the end of the tenancy?

   _____

   _____

2. One of the legal obligations of a landlord is to execute the transfer of peaceful possession of the premises to the tenant. Why is this important?

   _____

   _____

Chapter 9

Chapter 9 Renting or Owning a Home
Section 9.2 Buying a Home

 Note Taking

Directions As you read, write notes, facts, and main ideas in the Note Taking column. Write key words and short phrases in the Cues column. Then summarize the section in the Summary box.

Cues	Note Taking
• Real property includes buildings, fences, trees on surface; also soil, rocks, and minerals below ground. • Forms of co-ownership: • Types of deeds:	**THE NATURE OF REAL PROPERTY** • Real property is the ground and everything permanently attached to it. **TAKING OWNERSHIP** • Ownership comes through deed, inheritance, or law. **LIMITATIONS ON PROPERTY USE** • Zoning laws limit the way property can be used.

Summary
Real property is the ground and everything permanently attached to it.

Chapter 9 Renting or Owning a Home
Section 9.2 Buying a Home

 Reading Comprehension
Matching

Directions Match the letter of each type of co-ownership below with the correct definition that follows. Some answers will be used more than once.

a. tenancy in common
b. joint tenancy
c. community property
d. tenancy by the entirety
e. tenancy in partnership

_____ 1. A property is acquired by the personal efforts of either spouse during marriage. By law, it belongs to both spouses equally.

_____ 2. Each owner's share goes to his or her heirs upon death.

_____ 3. Each owner's share goes to the surviving co-owners upon death.

_____ 4. Partners have the right to use the property only for partnership purposes.

_____ 5. This property is held by a husband and wife, who have an equal right to the property. Each owns the entire property, which neither can transfer without the other's consent.

_____ 6. An owner may deed away ownership interest without permission of the other owners.

_____ 7. If a partner dies, the heirs inherit an interest in the partnership but not the specific real property.

_____ 8. Only nine states recognize this type of co-ownership.

Chapter 9

Chapter 9 Renting or Owning a Home
Section 9.2 Buying a Home

Study Skills
Improving Concentration

Directions Read the tips below. Then answer the questions that follow. If the statement is true, circle the letter *T*. If the statement is false, circle the letter *F* and write the correct version on the lines provided.

TIPS FOR IMPROVING CONCENTRATION
Improving concentration allows you to learn more at a faster rate.
• Remove or turn off all distractions in your study place, such as the radio, telephone, and television.
• Do not try to study for hours at a time. Take a break about every 20 minutes or so.
• When you feel yourself losing your concentration, close your eyes and take a few deep breaths. This will help you to relax and regain your concentration.
• While studying, remind yourself to concentrate on what you are reading. Avoid allowing your mind to wander or daydream as you read.

1. Ownership of real property can be lost by adverse possession.   **T F**

   _____

   _____

2. A lien is an irrevocable right to the limited use of another's land.   **T F**

   _____

   _____

3. A general warranty deed provides the grantee with no protection against   **T F**
   a faulty title.

   _____

   _____

4. Eminent domain is the right of the government to take private land for   **T F**
   a public purpose.

   _____

   _____

5. A license is a legal claim against another person's property as   **T F**
   security for a debt or loan to ensure it will be repaid.

   _____

   _____

Chapter 9

Chapter 9 Renting or Owning a Home
Section 9.2 Buying a Home

 Test Prep
Open-Book Tests

Directions Use these tips to prepare for an open-book test. Then answer the questions that follow.

PREPARING FOR AN OPEN-BOOK TEST
• Keep up-to-date on reading the text and studying your notes. You may use both the text and your notes in an open-book test.
• Make notes in the margins of your text and beside certain points you feel are important. This will help you locate them quickly during the test.
• Mark your notes with a highlighter. This will help you find important points quickly during the test.
• Condense your notes into only those that you want to use for the test. Do not overburden yourself with too many notes. Time is limited when taking a test, so being prepared and organized is important.

1. Why is it important to be prepared and organized prior to taking an open-book test?

   _____

   _____

2. Would you tell another student that an open-book test is easier or harder than a closed book test? Explain your answer.

   _____

   _____

3. What materials can be used in an open-book test?

   _____

   _____

4. How will it help you to highlight your notes?

   _____

   _____

5. How can making notes in the margins help you during the test?

   _____

   _____

Chapter 9 Renting or Owning a Home
Chapter Content Vocabulary

 English Language Arts
Writing

Directions Unscramble the words below. Then use each word in a sentence to show that you understand its meaning. The first one has been done for you.

nioticve	eviction
ttseea	
eedd	
eslea	
ublsaese	
ensceil	
nlei	
teninme namido	
nanytec	
erla ypporrte	

1. The landlord sent the tenant an eviction notice to vacate the premises. _____

_____

2. _____

_____

3. _____

_____

4. _____

_____

5. _____

_____

6. _____

_____

7. _____

_____

Chapter 9

Chapter 9 Renting or Owning a Home
Chapter Academic Vocabulary

 English Language Arts
Vocabulary

Directions Insert the word that best completes each sentence.

vacate	permission
assign	spouse
provision	consent

1. An easement cannot be terminated without the _____ of the owner.

2. If evicted, a tenant must _____ the premises.

3. As a tenant in common, an owner may deed away his or her interest without the

   _____ of the other owners.

4. Community property is property acquired by the personal efforts of either _____
   during marriage.

5. Many leases contain a(n) _____ allowing renters the option to renew the lease for
   one or more additional periods.

6. Some leases permit a tenant to _____ or sublet the property to someone else.

Chapter 10 Banking and Negotiable Instruments
Section 10.1 Using Negotiable Instruments

Note Taking

Directions As you read, write notes, facts, and main ideas in the Note Taking column. Write key words and short phrases in the Cues column. Then summarize the section in the Summary box.

Cues	Note Taking
• Maker: promises to pay	**TYPES OF NEGOTIABLE INSTRUMENTS** • Negotiable instruments help people to: • Types of notes: • Types of drafts: **TRANSFERRING NEGOTIABLE INSTRUMENTS** • Negotiation is the transfer of an agreement so that the transferee becomes the holder.

Summary

A negotiable instrument is a written document giving rights to others through indorsement or delivery.

Chapter 10

Chapter 10 Banking and Negotiable Instruments

Section 10.1 Using Negotiable Instruments

 Reading Skills
Creating a Table

Directions Use a word-processing program to create a table. First, read the instructions below. Then match the type of negotiable instrument (List A) with its function (List B) to complete the table.

1. Start up your word-processing program. Create a table with eight columns and nine rows.
2. In the top row, enter the types of negotiable instruments from List A. In the first column, enter the functions of negotiable instruments from List B.
3. Match each type with its function. Place an *X* in the box where the matching column and row intersect.
4. After completing your table, title it and save your work. Print out a copy of your table if your teacher has instructed you to do so.

List A

demand note
time note
installment note
certificate of deposit
sight draft
time draft
letter of credit

List B

not payable until a particular period of time has passed
used in international business
payable when given to drawee
payable when payee demands payment
payable at a future date
issued by bank, earns interest
paid in a series of payments

Type of Instrument →							
Function ↓							

Chapter 10

Chapter 10 Banking and Negotiable Instruments
Section 10.1 Using Negotiable Instruments

Study Skills
Listening Skills

Directions Read the tips below. Then answer the questions that follow.

IMPROVING LISTENING SKILLS
• Before class, skim the material your teacher will be talking about. This will better prepare you when you listen to the lecture in class.
• Try to anticipate what your teacher is going to say about the material. You may not always be correct, but this will prepare your brain to receive the new information.
• Keep the five W questions in your head: who, what, where, when, and why. Listening actively like this during class will help you retain information.
• Try to relate the material to something in your personal life. This will help you to better understand what you are hearing.
• Restate in your own words what your teacher is saying.
• Take notes while you are listening. After class, rewrite your notes and study them.

1. How does anticipating what your teacher is going to say help you listen better?

_____

_____

2. What should you keep in mind while your teacher is talking about the subject?

_____

_____

3. Why should you try to relate the material to something in your own life?

_____

_____

4. What should you do before, during, and after class?

_____

_____

5. What advice would you give another student about the importance of listening actively?

_____

_____

Chapter 10

Chapter 10 Banking and Negotiable Instruments
Section 10.1 Using Negotiable Instruments

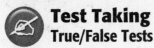
Test Taking
True/False Tests

Directions Practice the test-taking tips below while answering the questions that follow. Circle *T* if the statement is true. Circle *F* if the statement is false.

TRUE/FALSE TEST TIPS

- Answer *True* only when every part of the entire statement is true. If part of the statement is false, the entire statement is false. Watch out for long sentences that include a series or a list set off by commas or semicolons. Every part of the entire series must be true in order for the answer to be true.
- Most true/false tests have more true answers than false answers.
- Watch out for words that are unqualified, such as *always, never, every,* or *none*. These usually indicate a false answer. Most statements are not true all the time.
- Change the sentences written in the negative (*no, not, cannot*) to a positive by reading the sentence without the negative word. If the statement without the negative is true, then you know the answer with the negative is probably the opposite, or false.

---

1. Negotiable instruments are usually obtained from places such as banks and credit unions.　　　　　**T F**

2. In a draft, drawees are never required to pay money.　　　　　**T F**

3. People often sign an installment note when they borrow money to buy a car or a house.　　　　　**T F**

4. An instrument that has been written in pencil is never negotiable.　　　　　**T F**

5. If the date has been omitted from a check, the date on which it was received is considered the date of issue.　　　　　**T F**

6. Instruments that do not meet the requirements of negotiability cannot be negotiated.　　　　　**T F**

7. A negotiable instrument does not need to be for a specified amount of money.　　　　　**T F**

8. A negotiable instrument must be in writing, be signed by the maker or drawer, contain an unconditional promise or order to pay, be payable for a fixed amount, be payable on demand or at a definite time, and hold more than $200 in value.　　　　　**T F**

9. The four types of indorsements are blank indorsements, special indorsements, restrictive indorsements, and qualified indorsements.　　　　　**T F**

10. No person is liable on an instrument unless that person's signature appears on it.　　　　　**T F**

Chapter 10 Banking and Negotiable Instruments
Section 10.2 Banking Basics

 Note Taking

Directions As you read, write notes, facts, and main ideas in the Note Taking column. Write key words and short phrases in the Cues column. Then summarize the section in the Summary box.

Cues	Note Taking
• Check: most common type of negotiable instrument	**CHECKING ACCOUNTS** • A checking account creates a contractual relationship between bank and customer. **ELECTRONIC BANKING** • Electronic fund transfer (EFT) is a computerized system for transferring funds electronically rather than by written check.

Summary

The checking account is the most common type of negotiable contract.

Chapter 10

Chapter 10 Banking and Negotiable Instruments
Section 10.2 Banking Basics

Reading Comprehension
Analytical Skills

Directions In Section 10.2, you learned about the procedures and conditions for two types of banking: checking accounts and electronic banking. Decide which type is described in each statement or question below. Write "paper checks" or "electronic banking" on the line provided.

1. Care should always be taken to write checks so they cannot be changed easily.

   _____

2. Using a computer to view account balances and pay bills involves this type of banking.

   _____

3. Which type of banking allows one to purchase merchandise at a store with a debit card?

   _____

4. Money orders are drafts that substitute for checks and may be purchased from places such as banks and post offices. _____

5. With which type of banking is forgery or material alteration a threat? _____

6. Which type of banking permits one to authorize direct withdrawals from an account to pay bills automatically? _____

7. Traveler's checks, bank drafts, certified checks, and cashier's checks are used in this type of banking. _____

8. A stop payment may be issued by requesting a stop-payment order from the bank.

   _____

9. Using this type of banking allows one to make payments from the bank by telephone.

   _____

10. Which type of banking allows one to authorize an employer to deposit earnings directly into one's bank account? _____

Chapter 10

Chapter 10 Banking and Negotiable Instruments
Section 10.2 Banking Basics

Study Skills
Improving Learning Skills

Directions Read the tips below. Then answer the questions that follow.

IMPROVING LEARNING SKILLS
• Summarize a section after you read it.
• Ask yourself questions about the subject you are studying.
• Use different sources to obtain information about the subject.
• Use different methods to learn information. For example, read the text aloud. This stimulates more areas of your brain. You are learning both visually and auditorily.
• Find the conditions that are best for you. For example, join a study group, or find a quiet place if you study best alone.
• Think about other things you have learned and how you learned them. Did you learn by reading, having someone show you, looking at pictures and graphs, or listening to someone speak? Use these same ways of learning when studying new material.

1. Name something you have learned to do. Explain how you learned to do it.

_____

_____

2. How might understanding how you learn help you improve your learning skills?

_____

_____

3. How might summarizing a section after reading it help you learn?

_____

_____

4. How might asking questions help you learn?

_____

5. Why is it important to use different sources to learn? Name three sources you might use.

_____

_____

6. How might using different methods of learning at the same time help you learn?

_____

_____

Chapter 10

Chapter 10 Banking and Negotiable Instruments
Section 10.2 Banking Basics

Test Taking
Fill-in-the-Blank Tests

Directions Practice the test-taking tips below while answering the questions that follow. Fill in the blank with the best word choice from the list.

FILL-IN-THE-BLANK TEST TIPS
• Carefully read all the words in the list first. Think about what each word means.
• Carefully read each question.
• Fill in the blanks you are sure of with the best word choice. Some words may have similar meanings, so make sure you choose the best one.
• Cross off each word after you use it.
• Once you have eliminated the words you are sure of, review the words you are less sure of. Reread each question. Fill in the blank with the best choice.
• Check the list to make sure you have used all the words.
• Reread all questions to make sure you have answered each one.

debit card	money order
certified check	material alteration
checking account	statement
stop-payment order	outstanding check

1. A(n) _____ creates a contractual relationship between a bank and a customer.

2. Every month you should receive a(n) _____ of the bank's record of all your transactions.

3. A(n) _____ is a check you have written that has not been returned to the bank for payment.

4. A(n) _____ occurs when someone changes a check you wrote, such as adding an extra 0 to the amount.

5. A(n) _____ is a check that is guaranteed by the bank.

6. You can purchase merchandise at a store with your _____.

7. A draft that substitutes for a check and may be purchased from places such as banks and

   post offices is called a(n) _____.

8. You can put a stop on a check by requesting a(n) _____ from your bank.

Chapter 10

Chapter 10 Banking and Negotiable Instruments
Chapter Content Vocabulary

English Language Arts
Definitions

Directions Choose ten words from the list below. Use each in a sentence that shows you understand the meaning of the word.

payee	holder	electronic fund transfer
draft	assignment	indorsement
negotiable instrument	drawer	holder in due course
note	drawee	forgery
maker	negotiation	

1. _____

_____

2. _____

_____

3. _____

_____

4. _____

_____

5. _____

_____

6. _____

_____

7. _____

_____

8. _____

_____

9. _____

_____

10. _____

_____

Chapter 10

Chapter 10 Banking and Negotiable Instruments
Chapter Academic Vocabulary

 English Language Arts
Reading Skills

Directions Complete the graphic organizer below for each vocabulary term as you read the text. The first term has been done for you.

1	2	3	4	5
Read the Word	Rate the word: 0 = Do not know meaning 1 = might know meaning 2 = know the meaning	Predict the meaning before reading the text	Revise the meaning after reading the text	Write context clues
advantage	1	having the upper hand	a more favorable condition	Electronic banking has advantages over paper checks.
signature				
unconditional				
schedule				
reconcile				
substitute				

Chapter 11 Credit and Debt
Section 11.1 Understanding Credit

 Note Taking

Directions As you read, write notes, facts, and main ideas in the Note Taking column. Write key words and short phrases in the Cues column. Then summarize the section in the Summary box.

Cues	Note Taking
• Creditor: sells goods on credit or lends money	**CREDIT** • Credit: arrangement to receive cash, goods, or services now and pay in the future
• Security: a way for creditors to get money back in case borrower does not pay	• To obtain credit or loan: First, fill out application. **SECURED TRANSACTIONS** • Security interest created in two ways:

Summary
Open-end credit can be increased by continuing to make purchases.

Chapter 11 Credit and Debt
Section 11.1 Understanding Credit

 Social Studies
Sequencing Events

Directions Read the information in the box below. Then complete the chart that follows on the sequence of events in obtaining credit.

UNDERSTANDING SEQUENCE
A sequence of events shows the order of how something happens. Sequence explains what happens in the first step or event, and how that leads to the next step, and the next. Sequencing words such as *first, before, next, after, finally,* and *last* give clues as to the order of events.

Person fills out an application for credit or loan.

↓

↓

↓

Debtor pays off the credit.	Debtor defaults on the loan.

Chapter 11 Credit and Debt
Section 11.1 Understanding Credit

 Study Skills
Revising Notes

Directions Read the tips below. Then develop a note-taking plan that will work best for you. Write your plan on the lines provided. Share it with a classmate and exchange ideas.

REVISING YOUR NOTES
Taking notes in class and while reading the text is an important study skill. You can make your notes more useful by revising them after class or after you have finished reading the text. Here is how:

Recopy your notes. This helps you better organize your notes into main ideas and details. It also gives you an opportunity to make your writing neater and easier to read. Recopying notes is more effective than just reading them over. The information gets to your brain through a different path—your sense of touch. You can also process the information auditorily by reading your notes aloud as you recopy them.

Highlight or color code. After you recopy your notes, develop a system to color code the information. Highlight main ideas in one color and supporting details in another color. Do the same for important vocabulary words: Highlight the words in one color and the definitions in another.

Use graphic organizers. Recopy your notes into diagrams or visuals that help you organize and remember the information. This helps you see how ideas and information are related.

Use note cards. Recopy your notes onto separate note cards. Put a main idea on one side and the supporting information on the other. Use them like flash cards when you study.

_____

_____

_____

_____

_____

_____

_____

_____

_____

Chapter 11 Credit and Debt
Section 11.1 Understanding Credit

 Test Taking
Rewarding Yourself

Directions Read the tips below. Then answer the questions by filling in the
bubble next to the correct answer.

TIPS ON REWARDING YOURSELF
• When studying for a test, take a ten-minute break every hour. Reward yourself with a short call to a friend, playtime with a favorite pet, or a healthy treat. • Set an alarm or keep an eye on your watch so you do not go more than ten minutes or so. • Make plans for your next reward, which will come during the next study break. • After you have resumed studying, reward yourself with mini-breaks. During these breaks, close your eyes, stretch, and take a few deep breaths.

1. An arrangement in which a person receives cash, goods, or services now and pays for
   them in the future is called
   ○ interest.   ○ default.
   ○ collateral.   ○ credit.

2. Property that is offered as a security interest is called
   ○ interest.   ○ default.
   ○ collateral.   ○ credit.

3. A fee charged for lending money is called
   ○ interest.   ○ default.
   ○ collateral.   ○ credit.

4. The failure to make timely payments on a loan is called
   ○ interest.   ○ default.
   ○ collateral.   ○ credit.

5. A creditor's right to use collateral to recover a debt is called
   ○ a secured loan.   ○ an attachment.
   ○ a security interest.   ○ an asset.

6. A person who agrees to pay off a debt when the debtor defaults on a loan payment
   is called
   ○ a secured party.   ○ a guarantor.
   ○ a creditor.   ○ a surety.

Chapter 11 Credit and Debt
Section 11.2 Credit and You

 Note Taking

Directions As you read, write notes, facts, and main ideas in the Note Taking column. Write key words and short phrases in the Cues column. Then summarize the section in the Summary box.

Cues	Note Taking
• Need to know the following before purchasing a car: • Exact price of the car	**BUYING A VEHICLE** • When you are buying an automobile, you can pay cash to avoid paying interest, or you can borrow money to finance the car. **USING CREDIT CARDS** • Used for borrowing money, but with a high interest rate and late-payment fees **STUDENT LOANS** • Federal government provides loans for students based on need. **WARNING SIGNS OF DEBT PROBLEMS** • Can make only minimum payments on credit cards

Summary

Before purchasing a car, you should know the price of the car, the amount you are borrowing, the finance charge, the APR, and the total sales price.

Chapter 11 Credit and Debt
Section 11.2 Credit and You

 Mathematics
Drawing Conclusions

Directions Read the information in the chart below about purchasing a car. Then answer the questions that follow.

Purchase Price	$25,000
Down Payment	$7,500
APR	6.5%
Payment Period	4 years
Monthly Payment	$415.01

1. Imagine you are buying a car using the information above. What is the amount you will

   need to borrow to purchase the car? _____

2. What is the total cost of the loan for purchasing this car? _____

3. What is the finance charge for borrowing this amount? _____

4. What percent does the finance charge represent on the total cost of the loan?

   _____

5. How could you reduce the finance charge?

   _____

   _____

6. Do you think it is fair that it will cost you $2,420.48 more to purchase this car? Explain
   your reasons.

   _____

   _____

   _____

   _____

   _____

   _____

   _____

Chapter 11 Credit and Debt
Section 11.2 Credit and You

Study Skills
Creating Study Aids

Directions Read the tips below. Then team up with a classmate. Using the tips, create test questions based on Section 11.2 for your classmate to answer. Write the questions on the lines provided. Your classmate should create test questions for you as well. After taking the test, review each other's answers. Discuss whether the study tips helped you better understand the section.

CREATING STUDY AIDS
• Make an outline of your notes using only the main ideas.
• Make up questions using the headings and main ideas in the section. Answer the questions.
• Make a time line of important dates or other events covered in the section.
• Make flash cards of key words, academic vocabulary words, and important dates and events.

TEST QUESTIONS

_____

_____

_____

_____

_____

_____

_____

_____

_____

_____

_____

_____

_____

_____

Chapter 11 (side tab)

Chapter 11 Credit and Debt
Section 11.2 Credit and You

 Test Prep
Motivating Yourself

Directions Read the tips below. Then take the practice test that follows.

MOTIVATING YOURSELF
• Instead of studying for a test because you *have* to, focus on why you *want* to. Why do you want to study the material? You may want to study the material in order to learn more about an interesting subject, to get an A in the class, or to know enough to pass the test. • Brainstorm and make a list of reasons you want to pass the test. Write down as many reasons as you can think of. • Visualize the reward you will receive for passing the test. • As you begin studying, take a moment to visualize your reward. • Visualize the reward again during study time to motivate you to keep studying.

1. The cost of a loan in dollars and cents is called the
   - ○ annual percentage rate.
   - ○ interest rate.
   - ○ finance charge.
   - ○ total sales price.

2. The true interest rate of a loan is called the
   - ○ annual percentage rate.
   - ○ secority interest.
   - ○ finance charge.
   - ○ total sales price.

3. Before purchasing a car, you should know all of the following except
   - ○ the exact price of the car.
   - ○ the amount you are financing.
   - ○ how long it took you to save money for the down payment.
   - ○ the APR.

4. All of the following are warning signs of debt problems except
   - ○ missing loan payments.
   - ○ making only minimum monthly payments.
   - ○ paying the entire balance each month.
   - ○ borrowing money to pay off old debts.

Chapter 11 Credit and Debt
Chapter Content Vocabulary

 English Language Arts
Writing

Directions Fill in each blank with the correct vocabulary term.

annual percentage rate	collateral
credit	creditor
debtor	default
finance charge	interest
secured loan	security interest

1. _____ is an arrangement in which you receive cash, goods, or services now and pay in the future.

2. A(n) _____ is a person who buys goods or services on credit.

3. _____ is the fee a creditor charges for lending money.

4. A(n) _____ is one which is backed up by property that the creditor can take if the loan is not repaid.

5. A(n) _____ is a person who sells goods or services on credit.

6. _____ is failure to make timely payments on a loan.

7. A(n) _____ is a creditor's right to use collateral to recover a debt.

8. _____ is property that is offered as a security interest.

9. A(n) _____ is the cost of a loan in dollars and cents.

10. The _____ is the true interest rate of a loan.

Chapter 11

Chapter 11 Credit and Debt
Chapter Academic Vocabulary

 English Language Arts
Reading Skills

Directions Match each term with its definition. Write the letter of the term on the line next to its definition.

a. assets
b. acquired
c. effective
d. involve
e. unauthorized
f. subsidized

1. _____ not given permission

2. _____ obtained or became the owner of

3. _____ helped by means of making a grant of money

4. _____ in force or active

5. _____ anything owned that has value

6. _____ include or be part of

Chapter 12 Credit Protection and Bankruptcy
Section 12.1 Credit Protection Laws

 Note Taking

Directions As you read, write notes, facts, and main ideas in the Note Taking column. Write key words and short phrases in the Cues column. Then summarize the section in the Summary box.

Cues	Note Taking
• Repossession is when a creditor reclaims property if the debtor does not make payment. • CCPA: requires creditor to inform consumers of costs and terms of credit	**LAWS PROTECTING CREDITORS** • Historically, creditors have held more control in the debtor-creditor relationship, thus fewer laws exist protecting creditors. **LAWS PROTECTING DEBTORS** • Several laws have been created by the federal and state governments to protect consumers: • Creditor may deny credit for only three reasons:

Summary
The federal and state governments have passed laws protecting both creditors and debtors.

Chapter 12

Name _____ Date _____ Class _____

Chapter 12 Credit Protection and Bankruptcy
Section 12.1 Credit Protection Laws
 Reading Comprehension
Reading a Table

Directions Graphs and tables are visual aids that can help you learn. Information presented in the text can be summarized and put into a graph or table so you can view the information in a different way. In the table below, match each act with its definition. Place a check mark in the appropriate column.

	Fair Credit Reporting Act	Equal Credit Opportunity Act	Fair Debt Collection Practices Act	Fair Credit Billing Act	Consumer Credit Protection Act
This law makes it illegal to discriminate against credit applicants.					
This law makes it illegal to threaten debtors with violence when collecting debt.					
This law states that creditors must correct billing errors brought to their attention.					
This law grants individuals the right to know what is contained in their credit reports.					
This law requires creditors to inform consumers of costs and terms of credit.					

Chapter 12

Chapter 12 Credit Protection and Bankruptcy

Section 12.1 Credit Protection Laws

 Study Skills
Identifying the Main Idea

Directions Read the tips below. Then identify the main idea(s) in the two paragraphs that follow. Write your answers on the lines provided.

IDENTIFYING THE MAIN IDEA
• The main idea of a paragraph is stated in the topic sentence. Most often the topic sentence is the first sentence in a paragraph.
• Sometimes the topic sentence is the last sentence in a paragraph. If the first sentence does not tell you the main idea, look at the last sentence.
• In some cases, the topic sentence is in the middle of the paragraph. In such a paragraph, you can find the main idea only by reading the paragraph carefully and figuring out what it is telling you.
• It is possible for a paragraph to have no topic sentence. The main idea is not stated clearly in any sentence in the paragraph. That is because the main idea has already been stated in a previous paragraph. Find the main idea. Then go back and read the no-topic-sentence paragraph carefully to determine whether it supports the main idea.

1. There are only three reasons a creditor may deny credit: low income, large current debts, and a poor record of making payments in the past. If you are denied credit, under the ECOA you have the right to know why. If it is due to information in your credit report, you have a right to receive a free copy of the report. If you find inaccurate or incomplete information in the report, you have the right to dispute it and have it corrected.

   _____

   _____

   _____

2. To protect consumers, both the federal and state governments regulate the credit industry. Most states, for example, have set a maximum amount that can be charged for interest. A law restricting the amount of interest that can be charged is called a usury law. Laws created by the federal government to protect debtors include the Consumer Credit Protection Act, the Fair Credit Reporting Act, the Equal Credit Opportunity Act, the Fair Debt Collection Practices Act, and the Fair Credit Billing Act.

   _____

   _____

   _____

Chapter 12 Credit Protection and Bankruptcy

Section 12.1 Credit Protection Laws

 Test Prep
Preparing for a Test

Directions Read the tips below. Then take the practice test that follows.

PREPARING FOR A TEST
• Prepare for tests beginning on the very first day of class.
• At the end of each day, review what you learned by reading over your notes and asking yourself questions about the material. Reread any sections of the text you do not understand.
• At the end of each week, review what you learned that week.
• Review for several short periods at a time instead of one long period. This will help you feel more rested and thus retain information more effectively.
• Turn the main points into questions. Answer the questions.
• Make flash cards of vocabulary words and terms you are unfamiliar with. This will help you learn the meanings of unfamiliar terms so you are better prepared for the test.

1. What are two main points of Section 12.1?

_____

_____

_____

_____

2. What part of the section do you need to reread for better understanding? Explain your answer.

_____

_____

3. Why would it help to study in short periods of time rather than a long period?

_____

4. Turn this heading into a question: Consumer Credit Protection Act. Answer the question.

_____

_____

5. Why are flash cards useful in preparing for a test?

_____

_____

Chapter 12 Credit Protection and Bankruptcy

Section 12.2 Bankruptcy Laws

 Note Taking

Directions As you read, write notes, facts, and main ideas in the Note Taking column. Write key words and short phrases in the Cues column. Then summarize the section in the Summary box.

Cues	Note Taking
• Consumer Credit Counseling Service (CCCS) is a nonprofit financial counseling program.	**BANKRUPTCY** • The purpose of bankruptcy is to free debtors of debt accumulated through no fault of their own. **TYPES OF BANKRUPTCY** • Two types of bankruptcy: • Four types of bankruptcy proceedings:
• Four types of bankruptcy proceedings:	
	RESTORING CREDIT AFTER BANKRUPTCY

Summary
The purpose of bankruptcy is to free debtors of accumulated debts.

Chapter 12

Chapter 12 Credit Protection and Bankruptcy
Section 12.2 Bankruptcy Laws

 Reading Skills
Matching

Directions Match each type of bankruptcy with its definition. Some will be used more than once.

a. Chapter 7 bankruptcy
b. Chapter 11 bankruptcy
c. Chapter 12 bankruptcy
d. Chapter 13 bankruptcy
e. voluntary bankruptcy
f. involuntary bankruptcy

_____ **1.** This law allows family farmers to remain operational while creating a plan for debt repayment.

_____ **2.** This occurs when a debtor begins proceedings to eliminate or reduce the burden of debt.

_____ **3.** This law requires that individuals get credit counseling from a nonprofit agency before filing for bankruptcy.

_____ **4.** People who have too much income to file for Chapter 7 bankruptcy may be able to file for this type of bankruptcy.

_____ **5.** Creditors and the court must approve reorganization plans in this type of bankruptcy.

_____ **6.** This occurs when creditors begin bankruptcy proceedings instead of the debtor.

_____ **7.** Individuals filing for this type of bankruptcy must complete a course in financial management after filing.

_____ **8.** This type of bankruptcy states that 50 percent of a debt must result from farm or fishing expenses.

_____ **9.** This type of bankruptcy is also called the Repayment Plan.

_____ **10.** This type of bankruptcy is also called Reorganization.

Chapter 12 Credit Protection and Bankruptcy
Section 12.2 Bankruptcy Laws

Study Skills
Studying Your Textbook

Directions Read the tips below. Then answer the questions that follow by writing the letter of each correct answer on the line provided.

TIPS FOR STUDYING YOUR TEXTBOOK
• After reading a chapter in your textbook, reread such features as the section and chapter introduction and summary. This will help you to pinpoint the main ideas in the chapter.   • Read the end-of-chapter study questions. Skim the text to find specific details to answer these questions. These questions are designed to help you understand the content of the chapter.   • Pay close attention to any tables or graphs used. These are ways of condensing information into a graphic aid to make it visible and easier to understand. Take advantage of these visual aids.   • Read any feature articles or "Did You Know" sidebars. These usually appear in a box or shaded area. These features use the chapter information in a different context to help you better understand it.   • Always read any vocabulary lists at the end of the section or chapter. Make sure you know the definition of each term. Review the chapter if there are any terms you are unsure of.

1. Voluntary bankruptcy is when the _____ begins the proceeding.
   a. creditor   c. petition
   b. debtor   d. None of the above

2. An automatic stay goes into effect when _____
   a. debts owed exceed $3,000.   c. a petition for bankruptcy is filed.
   b. three payments are missed.   d. creditors feel it is appropriate.

3. Chapter 7 bankruptcy allows _____
   a. businesses to remain in business.
   b. farmers and fishing businesses to operate.
   c. individual debtors to develop repayment plans.
   d. individual debtors to discharge all debts and get a fresh start.

4. A bankruptcy filing remains on a debtor's credit report for up to _____
   a. ten years.   c. six months.
   b. life.   d. one year.

5. Chapter 11 bankruptcy _____
   a. lets family farmers and fishing businesses remain operational.
   b. allows businesses to reorganize their financial affairs and still remain in business.
   c. permits individual debtors to reorganize debts and develop repayment plans.
   d. is not available to businesses.

6. Chapter 13 bankruptcy is available to _____
   a. farmers.   c. individuals.
   b. fishing businesses.   d. corporations.

Chapter 12 Credit Protection and Bankruptcy

Section 12.2 Bankruptcy Laws

 Test Taking
Essay Tests

Directions Practice the tips below while answering the essay question that follows.

TAKING ESSAY TESTS
• Answers to essay questions do not necessarily require a lot of writing. Instead, you should use as few words as possible. Your grade is determined by how well you answer the question, not how long your answer is. • Give specific information and facts, cite details, and give examples to support your answer. • In the first paragraph, answer the question directly in a complete sentence. State what the main points of your essay answer will be. You should have two or three main points. • In the next paragraph or two, explain your main points by providing supporting details and examples. • In the final paragraph, summarize your main points. • Read what you have written. Check for spelling, punctuation, and clarity.

Who is eligible for Chapter 7 bankruptcy? What steps are involved in petitioning for Chapter 7?

_____

_____

_____

_____

_____

_____

_____

_____

_____

_____

_____

_____

_____

_____

Chapter 12 Credit Protection and Bankruptcy
Chapter Content Vocabulary

English Language Arts
Vocabulary

Directions Choose ten of the vocabulary terms below. Use each in a sentence that shows you understand the meaning of the term.

bankruptcy	Chapter 11 bankruptcy
voluntary bankruptcy	Chapter 12 bankruptcy
involuntary bankruptcy	Chapter 13 bankruptcy
Chapter 7 bankruptcy	repossession
garnishment	usury law
Fair Credit Reporting Act	Equal Credit Opportunity Act
Consumer Credit Protection Act	Fair Credit Billing Act
Fair Debt Collection Practices Act	

1. _____

_____

2. _____

_____

3. _____

4. _____

_____

5. _____

_____

6. _____

_____

7. _____

8. _____

_____

9. _____

_____

Chapter 12 Credit Protection and Bankruptcy

Chapter Academic Vocabulary

 English Language Arts
Reading Skills

Directions Fill in each blank with the correct term from the list below.

dominant	petition
exceed	alternative
impersonate	discharge

1. Debtors may be able to _____ debt through bankruptcy, meaning they are relieved from paying the debt.

2. An automatic stay goes into effect when a(n) _____ for bankruptcy is filed.

3. An adjusted repayment plan is an example of a(n) _____ to bankruptcy.

4. In their relations with debtors, creditors are the _____ party.

5. The Fair Debt Collection Practices Act stipulates that debt collectors are not allowed to _____ government officials or attorneys.

6. Garnishment of a worker's wages cannot _____ 25 percent of weekly take-home pay, except for certain amounts of support payments and taxes.

Chapter 13 Agency and Employment
Section 13.1 The Agency Relationship

 Note Taking

Directions As you read, write notes, facts, and main ideas in the Note Taking column. Write key words and short phrases in the Cues column. Then summarize the section in the Summary box.

Cues	Note Taking
• The person who authorizes someone to represent their interests is the principal.	**UNDERSTANDING THE AGENCY RELATIONSHIP** • Agency relationship is formed when one person represents another in a business transaction with a third party. **TYPES OF WORK RELATIONSHIPS** • Not all work situations involve a principal-agent relationship. **CREATING AN AGENCY RELATIONSHIP** • An agency relationship is formed when a principal and an agent agree consensually to an arrangement. • Three ways the law can create an agency relationship:

Summary
Agency is a relationship in which an agent represents a principal in a business transaction with a third party.

Chapter 13

Chapter 13 Agency and Employment
Section 13.1 The Agency Relationship

 Social Studies
Classification

Directions Classifying information helps you remember important details.
Below are three types of work relationships. Complete the chart to describe
each kind.

Principal-Agent	Proprietor-Independent Contractor	Master-Servant
Role of principal: the party who needs help	Role of proprietor:	Role of master:
Role of agent:	Role of independent contractor: performs task for proprietor using own tools, making own decisions	Role of servant:
Terms of relationship: Agent can legally conduct business on behalf of principal.	Terms of relationship:	Terms of relationship: Employer has a high degree of control over employee's time, place of work, tools, and methods.
Example(s) of agents:	Example(s) of independent contractors:	Example: Many employer-employee relationships are considered master-servant.

Chapter 13 (side tab)

Chapter 13 Agency and Employment
Section 13.1 The Agency Relationship

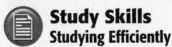

Study Skills
Studying Efficiently

Directions Read the tips below. Then answer the questions that follow. If the statement is true, circle the letter *T*. If the statement is false, circle the letter *F* and write the correct version on the line provided.

TIPS FOR IMPROVING EFFICIENCY

- Get yourself into a positive mood as you begin to study.
- Select the appropriate time, environment, and attitude.
- Mark any information you do not understand in a particular unit.
- Focus on one unit or a manageable group of exercises.
- After studying one unit, stop and write down what you have learned in your own words.
- Go back to what you did not understand and reconsider the information.
- Consult external sources such as other books or your instructor if you still cannot understand the information.
- Ask yourself these questions concerning the material you have studied:
  - What questions would I ask the author?
  - How can I apply this material to what I am interested in?
  - How can I make this information more appealing to my friends?
- Always review the material you have covered.

1. A person who authorizes someone to represent his or her interests is called a principal.   **T F**

   _____

2. The person with whom the agent does business on behalf of the principal is called the agent's agent.   **T F**

   _____

3. In a master-servant relationship, the person performing a task is the master.   **T F**

   _____

4. A gratuitous agent represents a principal for free.   **T F**

   _____

5. When a principal's actions lead the third party to believe that the agent is working for the principal, it is called agency by statute.   **T F**

   _____

Chapter 13 Agency and Employment
Section 13.1 The Agency Relationship

 Test Taking
What to Do During a Test

Directions Read the tips below. Then answer the questions that follow.

WHAT TO DO DURING A TEST
• Do not rush into the test right away. Read the directions carefully first. • Budget the time you have for taking the test. • Change your seating position to help you relax. • If you do not know an answer, skip it and go on. • If your mind goes blank during an essay test, just start writing. Ideas and answers will usually come. • Do not worry if other students finish the test before you do. Stick to your plan. • If you have time, go back to the answers you skipped and mark an answer, even if it is your best guess.

1. What are some strategies you can use to budget your time during a test?

_____

_____

_____

2. Brainstorm a list of things you can do to help you relax during a test.

_____

_____

_____

3. Brainstorm a list of things you can do when your mind goes blank on a question.

_____

_____

_____

4. Brainstorm a list of things you should do at the end of a test.

_____

_____

_____

Chapter 13 Agency and Employment
Section 13.2 Types of Authority and Agents

 Note taking

Directions As you read, write notes, facts, and main ideas in the Note Taking column. Write key words and short phrases in the Cues column. Then summarize the section in the Summary box.

Cues	Note Taking
• Power of attorney is any writing which grants someone authority to act as an agent.	**TYPES OF AGENT AUTHORITY** • Authority given to agents by principals may be actual or apparent. • Express authority includes three types of power of attorney: **TYPES OF AGENTS** • Type of agent is determined in two ways: extent of authority to perform tasks, and their relationship to other agents.

Summary
There are two types of authority: actual and apparent. Actual authority is the real power a principal gives to an agent.

Chapter 13

Chapter 13 Agency and Employment
Section 13.2 Types of Authority and Agents

 English Language Arts
Writing

Directions Write each of the five types of agents in the boxes below. Then write a characteristic of that agent on the line provided. The first one has been done for you.

| General Agent |

1. A general agent is an agent who has authority to perform any act within the scope of a business.

2. _____

_____

3. _____

_____

4. _____

_____

5. _____

_____

Chapter 13 Agency and Employment

Section 13.2 Types of Authority and Agents

 Study Skills
Learning New Material

Directions Read the tips below. Then answer the questions that follow.

LEARNING NEW MATERIAL
• Preview the material by scanning the table of contents, heading, and photo captions.
• Set your intention by thinking about what you want to learn.
• Break up the material into smaller sections.
• After reading a section, explain the information in your own words as if you were telling someone else.
• Reread any sections that are not clear to you.

1. Go back to Section 13.2. Scan the section and list what information you find.

_____

_____

_____

2. What should your intention be in reading the section again?

_____

_____

_____

3. How would you break this section up unto smaller parts to make it easier to read?

_____

_____

_____

4. Read the section again. Write a short summary of each smaller unit you created in question 3.

_____

_____

_____

_____

Chapter 13 Agency and Employment
Section 13.2 Types of Authority and Agents

Test Taking
Multiple-Choice Tests

Directions Read the information in the box below. Then take the practice test that follows. Write the correct answer in the space provided.

TAKING MULTIPLE-CHOICE TESTS
Multiple-choice items on standardized tests consist of a stem, or question, and distractors, or answer choices. Often, test takers read the stem, glance at the distractors, and quickly choose the answer they think is right. A better test-taking strategy is to read the stem and all the distractors before deciding. If you are unsure of the answer, eliminate the distractors that you know are not correct. Then decide on the best answer among the remaining choices.

1. Which of the following is not a type of agent?
   a. special agent
   b. general agent
   c. agent's agent
   d. new agent

_____

2. Which of the following is not a special agent?
   a. counterperson at a video store
   b. the owner of a company
   c. a pizza delivery person
   d. a car salesperson

_____

3. Which of the following is a type of power of attorney?
   a. a super power of attorney
   b. a limited power of attorney
   c. an apprehensive power of attorney
   d. None of the above

_____

4. Which is a type of agent authority?
   a. blatant authority
   b. constructive authority
   c. apparent authority
   d. zero authority

_____

5. Who appoints an agent's agent?
   a. another agent
   b. the principal
   c. a third party
   d. a coagent

_____

6. When apparent authority is based on previous dealings, what is it known as?
   a. implied authority
   b. assumed authority
   c. customary authority
   d. None of the above

_____

Chapter 13 Agency and Employment

Chapter Content Vocabulary

 English Language Arts
Writing

Directions For each word below, write one or two sentences to show that you understand its meaning. The first one has been done for you.

1. agency   In an example of the agency relationship, a grocery store owner is the principal, the employees are the agents, and the customers are the third party.

2. agent _____

_____

3. third party _____

_____

4. independent contractor _____

_____

5. actual authority _____

_____

6. implied authority _____

_____

7. power of attorney _____

_____

8. general agent _____

_____

9. subagent _____

_____

10. special agent _____

_____

Chapter 13

Chapter 13 Agency and Employment
Chapter Academic Vocabulary

 English Language Arts
Reading Skills

Directions Fill in the box at right with the best word from the list below. Then use the word in a sentence. The first one has been done for you.

genuine	apparent
conduct	incidental
gratuitous	extent

not fake or counterfeit **1.** The principal-agent relationship is a genuine agency relationship.	genuine
appearing as such but not necessarily so **2.** _____	
the point or degree to which something extends **3.** _____	
direct the course of, manage, or control **4.** _____	
complimentary; costing nothing **5.** _____	
accompanying; following as a consequence **6.** _____	

Chapter 14 Agency Authority and Termination
Section 14.1 Duties and Liability in Agency Relationships

Note Taking

Directions As you read, write notes, facts, and main ideas in the Note Taking column. Write key words and short phrases in the Cues column. Then summarize the section in the Summary box.

Cues	Note Taking
• Obedience: agent must obey all reasonable commands within the scope of the agreement	**AGENT'S DUTIES** • An agency relationship is a fiduciary relationship, which is based on trust. **PRINCIPAL'S DUTIES** • Four duties a principal owes an agent: compensation, reimbursement, indemnification, cooperation. **LIABILITY** • Determining who is liable depends on whether parties are principal-agent or proprietor-independent contractor. • Tort liability of principal: • Tort liability of proprietor:

Summary
An agent has a duty to a principal to be:

Chapter 14 Agency Authority and Termination
Section 14.1 Duties and Liability in Agency Relationships

📖 English Language Arts
Writing

Directions Read the information in the box below. Then write a Help Wanted ad to help the company find a qualified agent. Address all the duties of both agent and principal in your ad.

FAST ACTION VIDEO GAMES
Fast Action Video Games creates and manufactures popular computer games. The company is about to introduce a new line of games to the market. It is seeking a sales representative to sell the games to distributors nationwide.

HELP WANTED
Sales Rep for Fast Action Video Games, Inc.

_____

_____

_____

_____

_____

_____

_____

_____

_____

_____

_____

_____

_____

_____

_____

_____

_____

_____

Chapter 14

Chapter 14 Agency Authority and Termination

Section 14.1 Duties and Liability in Agency Relationships

Reading Comprehension
Compare and Contrast

Directions A foreign company that wants to do business in Israel can choose to contract with a commercial agent or with a distributor. Complete the chart below to compare and contrast the two choices. The first one has been done for you.

Commercial Agent	Distributor
Has the authority to act in the foreign company's name and can bind the company to any contract the agent feels is proper	Has only the right to market the products
Must follow any directives given by the foreign company	
	Not barred from selling competing products
Foreign company provides liability insurance.	
	Responsible for promoting the product of foreign company

Chapter 14

Chapter 14 Agency Authority and Termination

Section 14.1 Duties and Liability in Agency Relationships

Test Taking
Essay Tests

Directions Read the information in the box below. Then write a short essay explaining the differences between the duties of the principal and the duties of the agent.

TIPS ON ESSAY TESTS
Before you take a standardized or proficiency test, check to see if previous sample tests or previously administered tests are available to review. If so, look them over carefully to become familiar with the format of the essay portion of the test.   Read over each question and identify key words in the directions that tell you what to do. If the directions ask to *explain* something, your answer should go beyond a basic definition or list of information about the topic and include information and examples that tell why and how. If the directions ask to *compare and contrast* two things, you should describe similarities and differences. If the directions ask to *discuss* a topic, your answer should show that you have thought through all aspects of the topic or issue. Include specific examples and details to back up your main ideas.

_____

_____

_____

_____

_____

_____

_____

_____

_____

_____

_____

_____

_____

_____

_____

_____

Chapter 14

Chapter 14 Agency Authority and Termination
Section 14.2 Termination of Agency Relationships

 Note Taking

Directions As you read, write notes, facts, and main ideas in the Note Taking column. Write key words and short phrases in the Cues column. Then summarize the section in the Summary box.

Cues	Note Taking
• Impossibility of performance can happen if necessary subject matter is destroyed or if agent or principal becomes incapacitated or ill.	**TERMINATION BY OPERATION OF LAW** • Termination of an agency relationship by operation of law can occur when a major change affects the parties involved or alters the relationship's operation. **TERMINATION BY ACTS OF THE PARTIES** • Most agencies end when duties have been fully carried out by the parties. **GIVING NOTICE** • When agencies end, principal must notify all third parties who have done business with principal through agent. • Two types of notice:

Summary
Agency relationships can end by:

Chapter 14

Chapter 14 Agency Authority and Termination
Section 14.2 Termination of Agency Relationships

Study Skills
Managing Distractions

Directions Read the tips below. Then apply the tips as you read Section 14.2. Answer the questions that follow.

TIPS FOR MANAGING DISTRACTIONS
• Find a quiet place to study. Reading comprehension usually decreases in direct proportion to the amount of sound in a room. • If you cannot eliminate noise from your surroundings, try blocking it out with white noise. White noise is a bland, repetitive sound. Try turning on a fan or leaving your radio on a station where you hear only static. Your mind will get accustomed to the white noise and tune it out. • Certain kinds of music have the same effect as white noise. Easy listening or classical music sometimes can keep you from becoming distracted. • Get rid of inner noise. Eliminate worries, thoughts, and daydreams that keep you from concentrating.

1. Did your comprehension of the section improve by finding a quieter place to read? Why or why not?

   _____

   _____

2. Did your comprehension improve by creating white noise while you read? Why or why not?

   _____

   _____

3. Did your comprehension improve by listening to music? Why or why not?

   _____

   _____

4. Did your comprehension improve by eliminating inner noise? Why or why not?

   _____

   _____

5. What strategies worked best for you? Explain.

   _____

   _____

Chapter 14 Agency Authority and Termination
Section 14.2 Termination of Agency Relationships

Study Skills
Scheduling

Directions Read the tips below. Then answer the questions that follow by circling the letter of the word or phrase that best completes each sentence.

SCHEDULING YOUR TIME

- Take time to plan.
- Set realistic goals.
- Avoid marathon study sessions.
- Allow time for chores and errands.

- Do not forget to schedule time for fun.
- Plan a regular time for study.
- Stick to your schedule.
- Reward yourself.

1. An agency can end by operation of law, which includes all of the following except
   a. death of the principal or agent.
   b. bankruptcy.
   c. mutul consent or agreement.
   d. impossibility of performance.

2. An agency can end by acts of the parties, including
   a. death of the principal or agent.
   b. bankruptcy.
   c. completion of performance.
   d. impossibility of performance.

3. If an agent has an interest in the subject matter of an agency, the agency is
   a. irrevocable.
   b. mutual.
   c. compensatory.
   d. loyal.

4. The legal doctrine stating that the master is responsible for the torts of his or her servants is called
   a. fiduciary relationship.
   b. respondeat superior.
   c. double representation.
   d. indemnification.

5. Notice given directly to a third party, usually by certified mail, is called
   a. mutual agreement.
   b. completion of performance.
   c. notice by publication.
   d. actual notice.

Chapter 14 Agency Authority and Termination
Section 14.2 Termination of Agency Relationships

 Test Prep
Managing Stress

Directions Read the tips below. Then take the practice test that follows. If the answer is true, circle *T*. If the answer is false, circle *F.*

MANAGING STRESS
Have you ever experienced a sick feeling in the pit of your stomach before an important test, recital, or performance? Most people have. Have you ever been around other people who are experiencing stress? Did this add to your feelings of pressure? It is a good idea not to discuss your anxiety with others before a test.   Instead, monitor your own stress-related responses. Do you daydream, feel confused, have tense muscles, or feel you have a mental block? These are all responses to stress. You can manage these effects of stress by using relaxation techniques. Loosen any tight clothing. Close your eyes and take deep, slow breaths. Do stretching exercises. Curl your toes and hold for a count of ten, then relax. Repeat with the other muscles in your body, working your way up to your neck and face.

1. An agency relationship can be terminated by operation of law or by the acts of the parties. **T F**

2. When the parties have fully carried out their duties, the agency relationship is said to end by operation of law. **T F**

3. When the principal goes bankrupt, the agency relationship is said to end by the acts of the parties. **T F**

4. An agency relationship can be terminated if the agent or principal becomes incapacitated or ill. **T F**

5. Irrevocable agency means the agent may withdraw from the relationship at any time. **T F**

6. Notice by publication is usually sent through the mail. **T F**

7. An agency relationship will end through impossibility of performance if the subject matter of the contract is destroyed. **T F**

8. Bankruptcy gives a trustee title to the principal's property for the benefit of debtors. **T F**

Chapter 14

Chapter 14 Agency Authority and Termination
Chapter Content Vocabulary

 English Language Arts
Writing

Directions Match each word or phrase with its definition. Write the letter of the word on the line next to the definition.

a. self-dealing
b. compensation
c. double representation
d. fiduciary relationship
e. reimbursement
f. indemnification
g. respondeat superior
h. nondelegable duty
i. actual notice
j. notice by publication

1. _____ fair payment

2. _____ when an agent works simultaneously for two competing principals

3. _____ a formal notice given directly to a party

4. _____ payment for money spent by an agent on behalf of a principal

5. _____ a relationship built on trust

6. _____ payment for losses suffered by an agent because of a principal's instructions

7. _____ when agents make deals that benefit themselves rather than their principal

8. _____ a legal doctrine that states that the master is responsible for the torts of his or her servants

9. _____ a duty that cannot be transferred

10. _____ notice usually given by publishing a notice in a local newspaper

Chapter 14 Agency Authority and Termination
Chapter Academic Vocabulary

 English Language Arts
Reading Skills

Directions Fill in the blank with the correct vocabulary word.

loyal	benefit
adhere	mutual
cooperation	irrevocable

1. If a principal does not _____ to the duties set forth, he or she may be liable to the agent or third party.

2. Bankruptcy gives a trustee title to the principal's property for the _____ of creditors.

3. An agency relationship can be ended by _____ consent.

4. A(n) _____ agency means the agency cannot be revoked until the agent is paid fully.

5. Agents must be _____ to their principals.

6. If the principal interferes with the agent's performance, the principal has breached the duty of _____.

Chapter 14

Chapter 15 Employment Law
Section 15.1 Employment Agreements

 Note Taking

Directions As you read, write notes, facts, and main ideas in the Note Taking column. Write key words and short phrases in the Cues column. Then summarize the section in the Summary box. Use an extra sheet of paper if necessary.

Cues	Note Taking
• Union: organization of employees formed to promote the welfare of its members	**EMPLOYMENT-AT-WILL** • Each party should be free to end the employment relationship at any time w/o penalty. • Does not apply to: • In promissory estoppel, fired employee must prove four points: **UNIONIZED EMPLOYEES** • Government banned unions at first, but after Great Depression in 1929, government allowed unions to negotiate contracts through collective bargaining. • Collective bargaining: • Laws regulating union activity include:

Summary

The doctrine of employment-at-will states that:

Chapter 15

Chapter 15 Employment Law

Section 15.1 Employment Agreements

Social Studies
Time Lines

Directions The events in the box below each played a role in the history of labor unions in the United States. Place them on the time line according to the correct year. Briefly explain why each event was significant.

Wagner Act

Landrum-Griffin Act

Great Depression

Norris-LaGuardia Act

Taft-Hartley Act

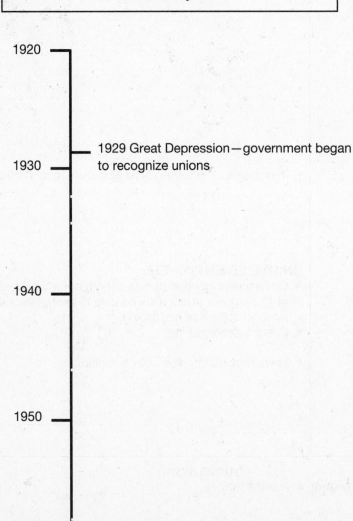

1920

1930 — 1929 Great Depression—government began to recognize unions

1940

1950

1960

Chapter 15 Employment Law
Section 15.1 Employment Agreements

Study Skills
Graphic Organizers

Directions Graphic organizers help group related information and make it easier to remember. Visual learners often use graphic organizers while taking notes in class or reading their textbooks. Complete the graphic organizer below by describing employment-at-will and its exceptions in the boxes provided.

Employment-at-Will

Exceptions to Employment-at-Will

Unionized Employees	Employment Contracts	Protected Classes

Chapter 15

Chapter 15 Employment Law
Section 15.1 Employment Agreements

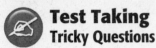 **Test Taking**
Tricky Questions

Directions Read the tips below. Then take the practice test that follows by writing the correct term in the space provided.

ANSWERING TRICKY QUESTIONS
Although some items on standardized tests can be tricky, tests are generally not designed to be so complicated or deceptive that they will fool all but the most wary of students. If you are worried that a question is misleading you or seems too easy, you are probably overthinking the question. Skip it and go on to the next question. Come back to the question later with a fresh approach.

1. An illegal contract that forces workers to agree not to join a union as a condition

   of employment is a(n) _____.

2. At least _____ of the workers must agree to contact the National Labor Relations Board to organize a full vote to form a union.

3. The _____ requires employers to negotiate wages, hours, and conditions of employment with unions.

4. The process in which unions and management negotiate wages and working conditions

   is called _____.

5. The legal argument that any employment relationship is based on an implied promise that the employer and employee will be fair and honest with one another is called

   _____.

6. _____ is a legal theory that permits a discharged employee to bring a wrongful discharge lawsuit against a former employer based on the argument that the firing hurts the public at large.

7. _____ bars an employer from taking back certain types of promises.

8. The doctrine of _____ is based on the principle that each party should be free to end employment relationships at any time without penalty.

Chapter 15

Chapter 15 Employment Law

Section 15.2 Employee Rights

 Note Taking

Directions As you read, write notes, facts, and main ideas in the Note Taking column. Write key words and short phrases in the Cues column. Then summarize the section in the Summary box. Use an extra sheet of paper if necessary.

Cues	Note Taking
• Employees have the right to: • health and safety protections	• Health and safety of workers protected by: • Fair wages and benefits protected by: • Privacy protected by: • Equal opportunity in the workplace protected by:

Summary
Government legislation regulates employment conditions to protect workers.

Chapter 15

Chapter 15 Employment Law
Section 15.2 Employee Rights

English Language Arts
Writing

Directions Read the tips below. Then write a paragraph or two describing the concepts of disparate treatment and disparate impact.

WRITING GOOD PARAGRAPHS
To make your writing more interesting and flow better, follow these tips. • Vary your sentence length. Make some sentences short and some long. • Use compound sentences—two sentences joined together with a comma or conjunction. • Use complex sentences—a sentence made up of an independent clause (a complete sentence) and a dependent clause. A dependent clause has a subject and a verb but is not a complete thought.

_____

_____

_____

_____

_____

_____

_____

_____

_____

_____

_____

_____

_____

_____

_____

_____

_____

_____

Chapter 15

Chapter 15 Employment Law

Section 15.2 Employee Rights

 Study Skills
Setting Goals

Directions Read the information in the box below. Consider what goals you would like to accomplish today, in the short term, and in the long term. Write them on the lines provided.

SETTING GOALS FOR SUCCESS
Good students set realistic goals to help them achieve. They create a plan for success and then work to make that plan a reality. • Make your goals clear, specific, and measurable. • Be sure your goals are realistic. • Phrase your goals positively. • Set a reasonable number of goals. • Think of achieving your goals as a game or challenge, not a chore. • Team up with a friend and encourage each other to reach your goals. • Be patient. Do not expect immediate results. • Have confidence in yourself. • Adjust your goals. Things change, and so can you.

Goals for Today

_____

_____

_____

Short-Term Goals

_____

_____

_____

Long-Term Goals

_____

_____

_____

Chapter 15

Chapter 15 Employment Law
Section 15.2 Employee Rights

Test Taking
Multiple-Choice Tests

Directions Read the tips below. Then take the practice test that follows by circling the letter of the correct answer.

MULTIPLE-CHOICE TEST TIPS

- Read the question and each answer choice carefully before making your selection.
- Be aware of negative words such as *not* or *opposite*. They are easy to skip over, causing you to misinterpret the question.
- Watch out for words such as *all, none, always, never,* and *every.* If you see one of these, try to find an exception to the statement before choosing your answer.
- Pay attention to answer choices that are long. The longest answer choices are often correct because they are carefully written and contain detailed information. If you are unsure of an answer, the longest answer is a good place to start.

---

1. Which is not an employment right?
   a. the right to health and safety protections
   b. the right to fair wages and benefits
   c. the right to discriminate
   d. the right to privacy

2. What is unemployment compensation?
   a. an insurance program that provides income for workers who are injured on the job or develop disabilities or disease as a result of their job
   b. a system of government payments to people who are out of work and looking for a job
   c. a program established by an employer or a union to provide income to employees after they retire
   d. a standard that states businesses must pay women the same as men for equal jobs

3. What is workers' compensation?
   a. a standard that states businesses must pay women the same as men for equal jobs
   b. a system of government payments to people who are out of work and looking for a job
   c. aprogram established by an employer or a union to provide income to employees after they retire
   d. an insurance program that provides income for workers who are injured on the job or develop disabilities or disease as a result of their job

4. Which act regulates the employment of minors?
   a. the Age Discrimination in Employment Act
   b. the Civil Rights Act of 1964
   c. the Americans with Disabilities Act
   d. the Fair Labor Standards Act

5. Which act prohibits discrimination in employment based on race, color, religion, sex, or national origin?
   a. the Age Discrimination in Employment Act
   b. the Civil Rights Act of 1964
   c. the Americans with Disabilities Act
   d. the Fair Labor Standards Act

Chapter 15

Chapter 15 Employment Law
Chapter Content Vocabulary

 English Language Arts
Writing

Directions Use at least ten of the vocabulary words below in a short essay that shows you understand the meanings of the words.

employment-at-will	equal pay rule
union	pension plan
implied contract	Social Security
public policy tort	unemployment compensation
implied covenant	workers' compensation
collective bargaining	discrimination
Occupational Safety and Health	disparate treatment
Administration (OSHA)	disparate impact

Chapter 15

Chapter 15 Employment Law
Chapter Academic Vocabulary
 English Language Arts
Reading Skills

Directions Use the words in the box below to complete the sentences that follow. Write the appropriate word on the line provided.

corruption	solicit
waiver	exceptions
voluntary	random

1. Some employees benefit from certain _____ to the employment-at-will doctrine that the courts have created recently.

2. The Landrum-Griffin Act amended the Wagner Act and is aimed at halting

    _____ in unions.

3. Employees who want to unionize must _____ workers, and at least 30% of the workers must agree to contact the National Labor Relations Board to organize a full vote to form a union.

4. The Environmental Protection Agency encourages _____ compliance by businesses.

5. The Employee Polygraph Protection Act prohibits the _____ testing of employees.

6. The Older Workers' Benefit Protection Plan helps workers remedy a situation in which

    they have been coerced into surrendering their rights by signing a(n) _____.

Name ______________________ Date ______________ Class ___________

Chapter 16 Forms of Business

Section 16.1 Sole Proprietorships and Partnerships

Note Taking

Directions As you read, write notes, facts, and main ideas in the Note Taking column. Write key words and short phrases in the Cues column. Then summarize the section in the Summary box. Use an extra sheet of paper if necessary.

Chapter 16

Cues	Note Taking
• States operate under either UPA or RUPA.	SOLE PROPRIETORSHIPS • Advantages: • Disadvantages: GENERAL PARTNERSHIPS • Advantages: • Disadvantages: • Partners share two types of liability: • Five types of partners: • Partnerships formed in two ways: • Partners share certain rights: • Partners have three duties: • Partnership may terminate as follows: • Other types of partnerships include: limited partnerships, limited liability partnerships,

Summary

A sole proprietorship is a form of business that is owned and operated by one person.

Chapter 16 Forms of Business

Section 16.1 Sole Proprietorships and Partnerships

 Reading Comprehension
Using a Table

Directions Use the table below to review the five types of partners. Place a check mark (✓) in each row that matches each partner with its definition.

	General Partner	Secret Partner	Silent Partner	Dormant Partner	Limited Partner
Liability does not extend beyond his/her investment					
Has active role in management and unlimited liability					
Does not play active role in management; is known to the public					
Plays active role in management; connection is kept secret					
Has no active role in management; is not known to the public					

Chapter 16 Forms of Business

Section 16.1 Sole Proprietorships and Partnerships

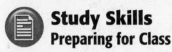 **Study Skills**
Preparing for Class

Directions Read the tips below. Then answer the questions that follow.

PREPARING FOR CLASS

Before Class
- Do your homework. While reading, try to form your own opinions about what is being said in the material.
- Review your notes from the previous day's lecture and reading.
- Communicate with your teachers about any questions you have about the material or any problems you are having with studying.
- Get a good night's sleep.
- On your way to class, get ready to focus. Take a moment to prepare yourself mentally for the day's topic.

In Class
- Arrive on time. It is disrespectful to your teacher and the other students when you arrive late.
- If there is open seating, position yourself so you can focus on the subject matter. Choose the best location for listening, asking questions, and seeing visual materials.
- Avoid distractions that may interfere with your concentration, such as daydreaming or dozing off. If you are feeling sleepy, start going to bed earlier.
- Evaluate the class material as you listen. Try to decide what is important, what you should include in your notes, and what can be left out. Listen long enough to make sure you understand what is said before you write it down.
- Make a to-do list that includes completing assignments, reviewing difficult concepts, joining study groups, and making appointments with a tutor or the teacher if needed.

1. What is one advantage partnerships have over sole proprietorships?

_____

2. What are the two ways in which a partnership can be formed?

_____

3. What are the five types of partners recognized by law?

_____

4. Name three disadvantages of a sole proprietorship.

_____

5. What are the three ways a dissolution of a partnership can happen?

_____

Chapter 16 Forms of Business
Section 16.1 Sole Proprietorships and Partnerships

Test Prep
Getting Organized for a Test

Directions Review the tips below. Then answer the questions that follow. If the statement is true, circle *T*. If the statement is false, circle *F*.

GETTING ORGANIZED FOR A TEST
• Begin reviewing several days before the test. This will give you more time to learn and become comfortable with the information.
• Start with short, daily review sessions, then progress into longer, more intense sessions as the test nears.
• Read all text assignments before each lecture. This will help you identify concepts that the teacher feels are important and may include on the test.
• Review your notes immediately after class. This will help reinforce the information while the lecture is still fresh in your mind.
• Review with a group of classmates. This enables you to cover important material that you may have overlooked on your own.
• Study the most difficult material when you are most alert.

1. A sole proprietorship is a form of business that is owned and operated by one person. **T F**

2. A sole proprietor must pay taxes as a business. **T F**

3. Partnerships may be formed by agreement or by proof of existence. **T F**

4. A liable partner is one of the five types of partners recognized by law. **T F**

5. Unlimited liability is a legal duty placed on a business owner that requires the owner to be responsible for all losses experienced by the business. **T F**

6. Joint liability is liability shared by two or more people. **T F**

7. Under RUPA, the three duties that partners have are loyalty, obedience, and trust. **T F**

8. A limited liability partnership is one in which all partners are liable for the acts of the other partners. **T F**

9. A joint venture is a business enterprise in which two or more participants combine in order to complete a single task. **T F**

10. A partnership is an association of two or more persons to carry on as co-owners of a business for profit. **T F**

Chapter 16 Forms of Business

Section 16.2 Corporations and Limited Liability Companies

 Note Taking

Directions As you read, write notes, facts, and main ideas in the Note Taking column. Write key words and short phrases in the Cues column. Then summarize the section in the Summary box.

Cues	Note Taking
• Share: single unit of ownership of a corporation	**CORPORATIONS** • Corporation is an entity with the legal authority to act as a single person, distinct from its owners. • A legal process is necessary to form a corporation: **LIMITED LIABILITY COMPANIES** • Limited liability company (LLC) is an entity with the legal authority to act as a single person, distinct from its owners, and combines the best features of a partnership and a corporation. **DOING BUSINESS INTERNATIONALLY** • Tax codes and laws differ in other countries.

Summary
A corporation is an entity with the legal authority to act as a single person, distinct from its owners.

Chapter 16 Forms of Business

Section 16.2 Corporations and Limited Liability Companies

 Reading Comprehension
Analytical Skills

Directions Answer the following questions by writing your responses on the lines provided.

1. Name the legal document that must be filed with the office of the secretary of state as a step in forming a corporation. _____

_____

2. What type of corporation includes incorporated political units such as towns, villages, and school districts? _____

_____

3. Name one advantage of a corporation. _____

_____

_____

4. Describe the role of the corporate promoter when forming a corporation.

_____

_____

5. What is the name for a corporation that is incorporated in another country but does business in the United States? _____

_____

6. Name one disadvantage of a corporation. _____

_____

_____

7. What is a person who owns shares of a corporation called? _____

_____

8. What must a corporation include in its name? _____

_____

9. What document gives a corporation official authorization to do business in a state?

_____

10. What is the term for a single unit of ownership of a corporation? _____

_____

Chapter 16 Forms of Business
Section 16.2 Corporations and Limited Liability Companies

 Study Skills
Paying Attention in the Classroom

Directions Read the tips below. Then answer the questions that follow.

PAYING ATTENTION IN THE CLASSROOM

- Try to anticipate the main ideas of the lecture by looking over your notes from the previous day's lecture and reading the course material.
- Resist distractions by sitting at the front of the room, away from disruptive classmates. Focus on the teacher through active listening and note taking.
- Maintain an attentive posture and expression. Do not slouch in your chair.
- Shift your position in your seat once in a while. Do not sit frozen in one position. Shifting will help your blood circulate and send more oxygen to your brain. This will help you to remain alert.
- Ask questions for clarity or when you are having trouble understanding the material.
- Train yourself to avoid distractions such as persons exiting and entering the room. Keep your concentration on what is being taught in front of you.

1. Describe the difference between share and shareholder.

_____

_____

2. What is the difference between articles of incorporation and a certificate of incorporation?

_____

_____

3. What are the three classifications of a corporation?

_____

_____

4. What is one advantage of a limited liability company?

_____

_____

5. What is expropriation?

_____

_____

Chapter 16 Forms of Business
Section 16.2 Corporations and Limited Liability Companies

 Test Prep
Tips for Better Test Taking

Directions Read the tips below. Then answer the questions that follow.

TIPS FOR BETTER TEST TAKING
• Prepare for tests by analyzing your past test results. Each test can prepare you for the next one.
• Arrive early for the test. Bring all the materials you will need, such as writing instruments, a dictionary, and a watch. These items will help you focus on the task at hand.
• Be comfortable and alert. If there is open seating, position yourself in a good spot where you have plenty of space to work. Maintain a comfortable posture. Do not slouch.
• Remain relaxed and confident. Remind yourself that you are well prepared and are going to do well. If you find yourself feeling stressed, take slow, deep breaths to relax.
• When you get the test, read the directions carefully first. This may seem obvious, but it will help you avoid careless errors.
• Look over the entire test before you start. Note key terms.
• Answer the easy questions first. This will help build confidence, score points, and mentally orient yourself to vocabulary and concepts. It may also help you make associations with more difficult questions.
• When answering the difficult questions, eliminate the answers you know to be wrong. This will increase your chances of choosing the correct one.
• Always review the entire test to make sure that you have answered all questions, that you have filled in the answer sheet correctly, and that you have not made other simple mistakes.

1. Why is it important to read the directions carefully before starting?

_____

2. What is a good strategy for answering difficult questions on a test?

_____

_____

3. Why is it important to review the entire test?

_____

_____

4. How can answering the easy questions first be a helpful strategy?

_____

5. What are some materials you should bring to a test? How will they help?

_____

Chapter 16 Forms of Business
Chapter Content Vocabulary

📖 English Language Arts
Writing

Directions Choose ten of the following terms. Use each in a sentence that shows you understand the meaning of the term.

sole proprietorship	dissolution	share
unlimited liability	dissociation	shareholder
partnership	limited partnership	articles of incorporation
joint liability	corporation	certificate of incorporation

1. _____

   _____

2. _____

   _____

3. _____

   _____

4. _____

   _____

5. _____

   _____

6. _____

   _____

7. _____

   _____

8. _____

   _____

9. _____

   _____

10. _____

   _____

Chapter 16

Chapter 16 Forms of Business
Chapter Academic Vocabulary

 English Language Arts
Reading Skills

Directions Complete the graphic organizer below for each vocabulary term as you read the text. The first term has been done for you.

1	2	3	4	5
Read the Word	Rate the word: 0 = Do not know meaning 1 = might know meaning 2 = know the meaning	Predict the meaning before reading	Write a new definition after reading. If the new definition is the same put a check mark in the column.	Write context clues
perpetual	1	ongoing, continuous	continuing forever; everlasting	Unlike sole proprietors, corporations have perpetual existence.
dormant				
incompetence				
domestic				
process				
similar				

Chapter 17 Operating a Corporation
Section 17.1 Managing a Corporation

Note Taking

Directions As you read, write notes, facts, and main ideas in the Note Taking column. Write key words and short phrases in the Cues column. Then summarize the section in the Summary box.

Cues	Note Taking
• Corporate directors must be reelected by shareholders.	**CORPORATE MANAGEMENT** • In a corporation, power is shared by many people:
• Shareholders have right to:	**RIGHTS OF SHAREHOLDERS** • Right to stock certificate: proves ownership
• Preemptive right: shareholder's right to buy stock before it is offered to the public	**LIABILITY OF DIRECTORS AND OFFICERS** • Business judgment rule:

Summary

Decisions for running a corporation are made by three groups of people—corporate directors, corporate officers, and corporate shareholders—who have certain rights and responsibilities.

Chapter 17 Operating a Corporation
Section 17.1 Managing a Corporation

 Social Studies
Careers

Directions There are many corporations in the United States. Some corporations manufacture products, others sell services. Think of a corporation you might like to work for. Write the name and a brief description of what it does in the box below. Then answer the questions that follow.

Corporation:

_____

Description:

_____

_____

1. What kind of position would you like to have in this corporation?

_____

_____

2. If you were a director of the corporation, what kinds of decisions would you make?

_____

_____

3. If you made a bad decision as director, could you be sued? Explain the rules the court would follow.

_____

_____

4. If you were an officer or director of the corporation, how could you get in trouble for insider trading?

_____

_____

5. What are some benefits of working for a large corporation?

_____

_____

Chapter 17 Operating a Corporation
Section 17.1 Managing a Corporation

Study Skills
Contextual Definitions

Directions Read the following tips and passage. Then write your own definitions for the terms below based on contextual clues in the passage.

USING CONTEXTUAL DEFINITIONS
Contextual definitions will help you understand the meaning of words you do not know and ideas that are hard to comprehend. Look for clues from the larger content of the text to help you figure out the meaning of unknown words or ideas. To read using contextual definitions, follow these steps: • As you read a passage in the text, circle unfamiliar words. • Reread the sentence a second time in which the unfamiliar word appears. • Focus on what you do understand in the sentence. It may help to reread the sentences before and after the one in which the unfamiliar word appears. • In your own words, state the meaning of the sentence. You may know only part of the meaning. State as much as you can. • Based on the meaning of the sentence, guess what the unfamiliar word means.

Forms of Business Ownership

The U.S. Small Business Administration (SBA) was created in 1953 as an independent agency of the federal government to aid, counsel, assist and protect the interests of small business concerns, to preserve free competitive enterprise and to maintain and strengthen the overall economy of our nation. We recognize that small business is critical to our economic recovery and strength, to building America's future, and to helping the United States compete in today's global marketplace. Although SBA has grown and evolved in the years since it was established in 1953, the bottom line mission remains the same. The SBA helps Americans start, build, and grow businesses.

1. independent: _____

2. enterprise: _____

3. critical: _____

4. global: _____

5. evolved: _____

6. mission: _____

Chapter 17 Operating a Corporation
Section 17.1 Managing a Corporation

Test Prep
Reducing Test Jitters

Directions Practice the tips below while answering the questions on the practice test that follows.

REDUCING TEST JITTERS
• It is normal to have jitters before and even during a test, so do not worry about those butterflies in your stomach.
• Remember, this is only one test. It may be an important one, but it is not the only test on which your grade depends.
• When you get jittery, take a deep breath. Count to three as you breathe in. Imagine the jitters are going out as you exhale.
• Get plenty of rest the night before a test.
• Dress in layers. If you get hot, you can remove a layer, or you can put one on if you get cold. It is important to be comfortable during a test so you can concentrate.

1. How does someone become a director of a corporation?

_____

_____

2. When a corporation has made a profit, must dividends to shareholders automatically be declared? Explain your answer.

_____

_____

3. How might shareholders who disagree with a decision of the board of directors go about defeating an issue affecting the corporation?

_____

_____

4. What does the corporate opportunity doctrine state?

_____

_____

5. What is the purpose of a shareholder's preemptive right?

_____

_____

Chapter 17

Chapter 17 Operating a Corporation
Section 17.2 Financing, Expanding, and Dissolving a Corporation

 Note Taking

Directions As you read, write notes, facts, and main ideas in the Note Taking column. Write key words and short phrases in the Cues column. Then summarize the section in the Summary box.

Cues	Note Taking
• Stock subscriptions: contracts to buy stock after a corporation is authorized to sell stock	**CORPORATE FINANCING** • Corporations need financing to pay for their business activities (e.g., research, product development, marketing, advertising). • Two types of stock: **CORPORATE EXPANSION** • A corporation can expand in several different ways: **DISSOLUTION OF A CORPORATION** • A corporation can be dissolved in two ways:

Summary
A corporation raises money by selling stocks or bonds.

Chapter 17 Operating a Corporation

Section 17.2 Financing, Expanding, and Dissolving a Corporation

 Mathematics
Reading Tables

Directions The table below identifies the fastest-growing franchises in the United States. Study the table and answer the questions that follow.

TOP FIVE FASTEST-GROWING FRANCHISES
Changes over a Five-Year Period

Franchise	Number of Units in the U.S.		Number of Units in Canada		Number of Units Outside North America	
	Year 1	Year 5	Year 1	Year 5	Year 1	Year 5
Subway	14,032	19,837	1,609	2,123	1,124	3,502
Pizza Hut	5,974	5,851	0	246	3,509	3,625
Quiznos	1,120	3,844	121	374	26	88
Jan-Pro Franchising Int'l. Inc.	1,170	3,918	96	188	0	0
Curves	3,130	7,879	295	736	0	0

1. Which franchise had the most units in the United States in the fifth year?

_____

2. How many more units outside North America did Pizza Hut have in the first year over Quiznos?

_____

3. Overall, which franchise has the most units globally in the fifth year?

_____

4. Which franchise has the least units globally in the fifth year?

_____

5. Which franchise decreased in number of units in the United States over the five-year period?

_____

6. Which franchise has the most units outside North America?

_____

Chapter 17 Operating a Corporation

Section 17.2 Financing, Expanding, and Dissolving a Corporation

 Study Skills
Using Both Sides of Your Brain

Directions Read the tips below. Then fill in the chart that follows by putting a check mark (√) next to each statement that is true.

USING BOTH SIDES OF YOUR BRAIN
Your brain has two sides. The left side controls logic, words, lists, numbers, sequencing, and analysis. The right side controls rhythm, imagination, daydreaming, color, size, and spatial awareness. Research shows that you have better memory skills if you use both sides of your brain. Try these exercises to help you develop both sides of your brain. • Stand straight. Lift your left leg forward. Touch your right hand to your left foot. • Lift your left leg behind you. Reach back and touch your right hand to your left foot again. • Now lift your right leg forward. Touch your left hand to your right foot. • Lift your right leg behind you. Reach back and touch your left hand to your right foot again. • Do things with your non-dominant hand, which is the hand you use less. For example, if you are right-handed, use your left hand to open doors, brush your hair, or write a column of numbers. If you are left-handed, use your right hand.

Corporate Expansion

	1. There is no significant difference between a merger and a consolidation, and the terms are often used interchangeably.
	2. General Electric owns financial services, plastics companies, and theme parks and is a good example of a sole proprietorship.
	3. A tender offer is an offer to end a corporation by a unanimous vote of its shareholders.
	4. McDonald's, Blockbuster, and Holiday Inn are well-known franchises.
	5. In an asset acquisition, a corporation buys the assets of another corporation rather than the corporation itself to avoid taking on the debts and liabilities of the other corporation.
	6. A business that buys a franchise benefits from the trade name and expertise of the parent company.
	7. Tender offers are often referred to as takeover bids.
	8. In a merger, both companies joined together are able to keep their corporate identities.
	9. A conglomerate is a corporation that specializes in one type of product or service.
	10. A corporation's assets include property, buildings, and equipment.

Chapter 17 Operating a Corporation
Section 17.2 Financing, Expanding, and Dissolving a Corporation

 Test Taking
Taking a Test

Directions Read the tips below. Then answer the questions that follow by writing the correct answer in the space provided.

TAKING A TEST
• Before you begin, read the test directions carefully. Underline words that will help you follow directions, such as *summarize, compare and contrast,* or *explain your answer.* • When you have completed the test, check your answers to make sure you answered every question. • For essay and short-answer questions, reread your answers. Make sure all words are spelled correctly, proper grammar is used, and sentence structure is correct.

1. Name some reasons why a government would dissolve or terminate a corporation.

_____

_____

_____

2. How does a broker fill a purchaser's order?

_____

_____

_____

3. If a corporation ends voluntarily, to whom must the dissolution be reported?

_____

_____

_____

4. What are stock subscriptions?

_____

_____

5. How are bonds different from stocks?

_____

_____

_____

Chapter 17

Chapter 17 Operating a Corporation
Chapter Content Vocabulary

 English Language Arts
Definitions

Directions Match each vocabulary word(s) with its definition below. Write the letter of the word(s) on the line next to the matching definition.

a. corporate director
b. corporate officer
c. direct suit
d. class action suit
e. derivative suit
f. insider trading

g. merger
h. consolidation
i. conglomerate
j. asset acquisition
k. stock acquisition
l. franchise

1. _____ The joining together of two companies, with one company keeping its corporate identity and the other losing its corporate identity.

2. _____ A person chosen by the directors to run the day-to-day affairs of a corporation.

3. _____ Two or more companies joining together to form a new corporation.

4. _____ One company agreeing to purchase the assets of a second corporation.

5. _____ A person elected by the shareholders to make broad policy decisions in the running of a corporation.

6. _____ A license a company grants to a business or individual to use its name and sell its products or services.

7. _____ When an individual or corporation buys enough shares of stock in another corporation to take over control of it.

8. _____ A lawsuit a shareholder can bring on behalf of the corporation to correct an injury to the corporation.

9. _____ A lawsuit shareholders with a common claim can bring as a group against a corporation.

10. _____ A corporate director or officer buys or sells shares in a corporation based on firsthand information about the corporation that is not available to the public.

11. _____ A corporation that owns many different types of companies.

12. _____ A lawsuit a shareholder can bring against a corporation for denying his or her rights as a shareholder.

Chapter 17

Chapter 17 Operating a Corporation

Chapter Academic Vocabulary

 English Language Arts
Reading Skills

Directions Choose the word in the box that correctly completes each sentence below.

proportionate	preemptive
exploit	subscription
significant	unanimous

1. Shareholders have the right to buy a(n) _____ share of every new stock issue before it is offered to the public.

2. Directors and officers must not _____ their positions for personal gain at the expense of the corporation.

3. A stock _____ is a contract to buy stock once the corporation is authorized to sell stock to the public.

4. There is no _____ difference between a merger and a consolidation.

5. A(n) _____ vote of its shareholders can voluntarily end a corporation.

6. The purpose of a shareholder's _____ right is to prevent the directors from taking control of the corporation by issuing more shares and buying them all themselves.

Chapter 18 Business and Regulations

Section 18.1 Corporate Regulations

 Note Taking

Directions As you read, write notes, facts, and main ideas in the Note Taking column. Write key words and short phrases in the Cues column. Then summarize the section in the Summary box.

Cues	Note Taking
• Government regulates commerce in three areas: securities, antitrust, corporate takeovers.	**BUSINESS AND THE CONSTITUTION** • The Commerce Clause of the U.S. Constitution gives Congress the power to regulate commerce among the states.

Summary

The Commerce Clause is a statement in Article I of the Constitution giving Congress the power to regulate commerce among the states.

Chapter 18 Business and Regulations

Section 18.1 Corporate Regulations

Social Studies
Regulating Business

Directions Governments regulate commerce in three areas: securities, antitrust, and corporate takeovers. Read the following questions and statements. Use the space provided to write which act of law each refers to. The first one has been done for you.

1. This antitrust law made monopolies illegal.

   The Sherman Antitrust Act _____

   _____

2. Which securities regulation was designed to protect investors by making sure they can learn about the securities they buy?

   _____

   _____

3. This law created the Securities and Exchange Commission.

   _____

   _____

4. This antitrust law makes it illegal to sell goods on the condition that a buyer cannot buy products from a competitor.

   _____

   _____

5. Which securities regulation prohibits most corporate loans to directors and executives?

   _____

6. Which federal regulation of corporate takeover acts requires a suitor to file a statement indicating where the money for the takeover is coming from, why the suitor is purchasing the stock, and how much of the target the suitor owns?

   _____

   _____

7. This antitrust law says companies cannot sell goods at lower prices to large purchasers without offering the same discount to smaller purchasers.

   _____

   _____

Chapter 18

Chapter 18 Business and Regulations
Section 18.1 Corporate Regulations

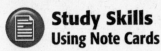

Study Skills
Using Note Cards

Directions Read the tips below. Then create your own note cards by using the model shown.

CREATING NOTE CARDS

When it comes to organizing your research for a project or paper, note cards can be useful. You can create cards from blank 3×5 or 5×7 index cards. Write information on them that pertains to the subject you are studying.

Topic:	Source:
Fact, quote, or thought:	

- In the upper left corner, write the topic of your paper.
- In the upper right corner, write the name of the source for this particular card.
- Enter a single fact, quote, or thought that you would like to include in your paper. Repeat with the remaining cards for each fact, quote, or thought.
- Organize your cards to coincide with the outline of your paper.
- Keep a separate set of cards for each type of resource you have used, such as magazines, Internet sources, textbooks, and other books.

Follow the model and create your own note card using the *BusinessWeek News* article in Section 18.1 of your textbook.

Topic:	Source:
Thought:	

Chapter 18

Chapter 18 Business and Regulations
Section 18.1 Corporate Regulations

Test Prep
Test Materials

Directions Read the tips below. Then answer the questions that follow by circling the letter of the correct answer.

ANTICIPATING TEST MATERIAL

- Pay special attention to study guides that your teacher has handed out.
- Do not be afraid to ask your teacher what material will be on the test.
- Pay close attention to points that your teacher brings up during class lectures just before the exam.
- Make a list of possible questions you would ask if you were writing the test. Try to answer your own questions.
- Review past tests.
- Confer with your classmates and try to predict what will be on the test.
- Be sure to note ideas or points that your teacher writes on the board or says more than once.

1. A business situation in which one person, company, or group of companies controls the market for a product or service is called
   a. a conglomerate.
   b. a successful business.
   c. a monopoly.
   d. a product regulation.

2. The registration statement is
   a. a general description of the securities and of the company making the offer.
   b. a federal regulation that makes selling goods across state lines illegal.
   c. a strict environmental regulation passed in 1933.
   d. a document that prohibits companies from selling goods at discounted prices.

3. A monetary investment that seeks to make a profit solely because of another's efforts is called
   a. a trust.
   b. a security.
   c. a monopoly.
   d. a commerce clause.

4. A statement in Article I of the Constitution giving Congress the power to regulate commerce among states is called
   a. the Securities Act of 1933.
   b. the Commerce Clause.
   c. the Sherman Antitrust Act.
   d. the Clayton Antitrust Act.

5. The Robinson-Patman Act is an amendment to
   a. the Federal Trade Commission Act.
   b. the Sherman Antitrust Act.
   c. the Clayton Antitrust Act.
   d. the Securities Act of 1933.

Chapter 18

Chapter 18 Business and Regulations
Section 18.2 Environmental Laws

 Note Taking

Directions As you read, write notes, facts, and main ideas in the Note Taking
column. Write key words and short phrases in the Cues column. Then summarize
the section in the Summary box.

Cues	Note Taking
• EPA = Environmental Protection Agency; established 1969	**ENVIRONMENTAL PROTECTION** • Industrial damage to the environment and human health caused government to pass laws protecting the environment. • Clean Water Act guards against water pollution. **ENERGY REGULATION AND CONSERVATION** • In response to the 1973 oil crisis, the U.S. government established the DOE.

Summary
The Environmental Protection Agency (EPA) is the federal agency responsible for protecting the environment.

Chapter 18

Chapter 18 Business and Regulations
Section 18.2 Environmental Laws

 English Language Arts
Reading Skills

Directions Read the tips below. Practice the tips while you read section 18.2 in
your textbook, then answer the questions that follow.

TIPS FOR READING DIFFICULT MATERIAL
• Begin by scanning the section. Look at titles, headings, and subheadings. Pay attention to graphs, charts, and diagrams.
• If there is an end-of-section summary, read it to familiarize yourself with the material in the section.
• Go back and read the section from the beginning. Highlight material that you do not understand so you can review it later.
• As you read, pause occasionally and ask yourself questions about the material you have just read. Make sure you can answer the questions before moving on.
• As you come across words you are unfamiliar with, stop and look them up in a dictionary so you can better understand what you are reading.
• If you have read the section and still do not understand parts of it, put it aside and reread it later. The material often will become clearer to you the second time you read it.
• If you have reread the material and are still having trouble, consult a classmate, teacher, or tutor for help.

1. What parts of the section were easy for you to understand? Which parts did you highlight
   and read a second time?

   _____

   _____

2. Which words in the section did you need to look up?

   _____

   _____

3. Which section headings or subheadings were most helpful to you while scanning the
   section?

   _____

   _____

4. Which parts of the section did you set aside to reread later?

   _____

   _____

Chapter 18 Business and Regulations
Section 18.2 Environmental Laws

Study Skills
Improving Your Study Habits

Directions Learn to implement these study habits below into your daily routine. Then answer the questions that follow.

TIPS FOR IMPROVING YOUR STUDY HABITS
• Take responsibility for yourself. Recognize that in order to succeed, you must make the right decisions about your priorities, time, and resources.
• Do not allow friends to influence you in a negative way about what you feel is important.
• Complete the goals you have set for yourself. Stay on task. Do not let friends or others distract you from your studies.
• Establish the time of day in which you study most effectively: morning, afternoon, or evening. Also, know the place that suits you best for studying. It may be your bedroom, the library, or some other location.
• If you are having trouble understanding the material, do not just keep reading it over and over. Ask another student or your teacher to help clarify for you.
• Challenge yourself continuously to improve your study skills and ultimately your grades!

1. What must you do in order to succeed in your studies?

_____

_____

2. How can you complete the goals you have set for yourself?

_____

_____

3. How can you maximize the effectiveness of your study time?

_____

_____

4. What strategy can you use when you are having trouble understanding the course material?

_____

_____

5. What advice would you give other students who are attempting to improve their study habits?

_____

_____

_____

Chapter 18 Business and Regulations
Section 18.2 Environmental Laws

 Test Prep
Review Tools for Tests

Directions Read the tips below. Then answer the questions that follow by writing the correct answer in the space provided.

REVIEW TOOLS FOR TESTS
• Create study checklists. Identify all of the material that you will be tested on. List notes, formulas, ideas, and text assignments you are accountable for.   • Make summary notes. These should display lists and hierarchies of ideas.   • Record class lectures and portions of the text you feel are important. Listen to them multiple times.   • Create flash cards for key terms and ideas that you need to memorize. Put the term or topic on one side of the card. Put the definition or description on the other side.

1. In what year was the Environmental Protection Agency established?
   a. 1900
   b. 1925
   c. 1969
   d. 2006

   _____

2. Which of the following is a role of the Federal Energy Regulatory Commission?
   a. dissolve monopolies
   b. regulate electricity and natural gas
   c. regulate nuclear energy
   d. regulate interstate trade

   _____

3. Which of the following was a result of the Clean Air Act of 1970?
   a. automobiles identified as a major source of air pollution
   b. the National Ambient Air Quality Standards
   c. government regulation of the auto industry
   d. introduction of the Kyoto Protocols

   _____

4. The Environmental Protection Agency can do all of the following except
   a. conduct research
   b. create and administer pollution control guidelines
   c. administer grants to help eliminate pollution under state-run programs
   d. control the wholesale price of natural gas

Chapter 18 Business and Regulations
Chapter Content Vocabulary

English Language Arts
Writing

Directions Use each of the following words in a sentence that shows you understand the meaning of the word.

Commerce Clause
security
registration statement
prospectus
monopoly
Environmental Protection Agency
Federal Energy Regulatory Commission
Nuclear Regulatory Commission

1. _____

_____

2. _____

_____

3. _____

_____

4. _____

_____

5. _____

_____

6. _____

_____

7. _____

_____

8. _____

_____

Chapter 18

Chapter 18 Business and Regulations
Chapter Academic Vocabulary

English Language Arts
Reading Skills

Directions Circle the letter for the term or phrase that best completes each sentence.

1. **Commerce** is
   a. the trading of something of value between two entities.
   b. a monetary investment that seeks to make a profit because of another's efforts.
   c. cooperation between state and national agencies to clean up waterways.
   d. regulated by the EPA.

2. **Administer** means
   a. to attend with regularity.
   b. to work in an administrative capacity.
   c. to work collectively.
   d. to work individually.

3. **Certify** means
   a. to be sure of.
   b. to fluctuate with irregularity.
   c. to guarantee as meeting a certain standard.
   d. to know to be accurate.

4. The EPA prefers that businesses follow or _____ with its standards.
   a. interfere
   b. tamper
   c. argue
   d. comply

5. The Clean Air Act of 1963 set automobile _____ standards.
   a. safety
   b. emissions
   c. color
   d. price

6. Being **proactive** means
   a. to work as much as possible.
   b. to present gifts to the EPA.
   c. to act before a situation becomes a source of confrontation or crisis.
   d. to react to a dangerous situation.

Chapter 19 Cyberlaw and E-Commerce
Section 19.1 Cyberlaw and Cybercrime

 Note Taking

Directions As you read, write notes, facts, and main ideas in the Note Taking column. Write key words and short phrases in the Cues column. Then summarize the section in the Summary box.

Cues	Note Taking
• Cyberlaw also called computer law, electronic law, e-law	**CYBERCRIME** • Cyberlaw: area of law concerning computers and computer-related crimes • Cybercrimes include crimes directed at people using computers and at other computers. **CYBERTORTS** • A cybertort is the use of a computer to commit a tort. • Two most common cybertorts are:

Summary
Cyberlaw is the area of law which concerns computers and computer-related crimes.

Chapter 19

Chapter 19 Cyberlaw and E-Commerce
Section 19.1 Cyberlaw and Cybercrime

 Reading Comprehension
Matching

Directions Match each cybercrime or cybertort with its definition. Write the letter of the term on the line next to its matching definition.

a. cyberspoofing
b. cyberpiracy
c. cyberblackmail
d. identity theft
e. cyberterrorism
f. cybervandalism
g. cybergerm warfare
h. cyberdefamation
i. cyberinvasion of privacy

_____ 1. adopting the identity of another computer user or creating a false identity to commit fraud

_____ 2. communication via computer of false data that damages a person's reputation

_____ 3. disrupting, damaging, or destroying a Web site or computer network

_____ 4. using illegally obtained information from a computer to pressure a victim into granting a payoff

_____ 5. using a computer to steal financial, employment, educational, medical, and personal data

_____ 6. transmitting computer viruses to destroy computer systems or files

_____ 7. unwelcome intrusion by computer into the private matters of an individual

_____ 8. using a computer to disrupt the national electronic infrastructure

_____ 9. using a computer to steal data

Chapter 19

Chapter 19 Cyberlaw and E-Commerce
Section 19.1 Cyberlaw and Cybercrime

Study Skills
Staying Healthy

Directions Read the tips below. Then answer the questions that follow.

TIPS FOR STAYING HEALTHY
Staying healthy will improve your ability to learn. Follow these tips to help maintain your physical, mental, and emotional well-being.   • Keep your mind active by reading, working math problems or crossword puzzles, or playing games.   • Exercise regularly to keep oxygen moving to your brain and throughout your body.   • Keep your stress level low. When you feel stressed, take a few deep breaths, talk to an understanding friend, or go for a walk.   • Talk to a parent or other wise adult, a teacher, or a school counselor if you are depressed.   • Stay away from alcohol and drugs of all types, including cigarettes.   • Participate in stimulating discussions with friends and family members.

1. What do you do to stay healthy? List the practices and activities that keep your mind and body in tip-top shape.

   _____

   _____

2. What benefits do your healthy practices provide you?

   _____

   _____

3. What practices and activities do you do that are unhealthy?

   _____

   _____

4. What benefits, if any, do your unhealthy practices provide you? Explain your answer.

   _____

   _____

5. What can you do to make your mind and body healthier? Develop a plan for the next four weeks to become a healthier person.

   _____

   _____

   _____

Chapter 19

Chapter 19 Cyberlaw and E-Commerce
Section 19.1 Cyberlaw and Cybercrime

 Test Taking
Short-Answer Tests

Directions Read the tips below for taking short-answer tests. Then answer the practice test questions below.

TAKING SHORT-ANSWER TESTS
• Read the question carefully. Look for key words and facts. • On another piece of paper, jot down notes about the facts and important information for your answer. • Organize your notes. • Write two or three short sentences. • Pack as much information as possible into your answer.

1. What is the difference between a cybercrime and a cybertort?

_____

_____

_____

2. Provide two examples of cybercrime. Explain what each is.

_____

_____

_____

3. Explain the difference between identity theft and cyberinvasion of privacy.

_____

_____

_____

4. List as many examples of cyberspoofing as you can think of.

_____

_____

_____

Chapter 19 Cyberlaw and E-Commerce
Section 19.2 Internet Transactions

 Note Taking

Directions As you read, write notes, facts, and main ideas in the Note Taking
column. Write key words and short phrases in the Cues column. Then summarize
the section in the Summary box.

Cues	Note Taking
• E-commerce = electronic commerce	**E-COMMERCE LAWS** • E-commerce is the process of conducting business using electronic means, especially the Internet. • E-commerce has raised several legal issues: **INTELLECTUAL PROPERTY** • Copyrights: **CYBERCONTRACT LAW** • Deals with the buying and selling of computers and computer programs

Summary
E-commerce is the process of conducting business using electronic means such as the Internet. E-commerce has raised jurisdiction, taxation, and authentication issues.

Chapter 19

Chapter 19 Cyberlaw and E-Commerce
Section 19.2 Internet Transactions

Reading Comprehension
Critical Thinking

Directions Read the tips below. Then answer the questions that follow.

CRITICAL-THINKING TIPS
Critical thinking allows you to understand what you read beyond the literal level. Critical thinking goes beyond the memorization of facts. It helps you to use those facts to draw conclusions; make generalizations, judgments, predictions, and inferences; and form your own opinions. Critical thinking involves: • Applying new things you have learned to what you already know • Using logical reasoning based on clues in what you have read • Making judgments about information • Looking for and understanding unstated ideas in the text

1. Currently, the courts have ruled that sellers who do not have a store, office, or wholesale shop within a state cannot be taxed by that state. That means a store that sells CDs over the Internet does not pay taxes to the state even though it sells CDs in the state. However, a brick-and-mortar store that sells CDs in a shopping mall pays taxes to the state in which it is located. Do you think the Internet store should also pay taxes to the state? Explain your answer.

_____

_____

_____

_____

_____

2. Copyright laws prohibit the illegal duplication of intellectual property. However, duplicating music from CDs for personal use has become common. Do you think this duplication is a violation of the copyright laws? Why or why not?

_____

_____

_____

_____

_____

Chapter 19

Chapter 19 Cyberlaw and E-Commerce
Section 1.2 Internet Transactions
Study Skills
Improving Memory

Directions Read the tips below. Then answer the questions that follow by writing the word(s) that completes the statement.

TIPS ON IMPROVING YOUR MEMORY
• Focus on remembering what you are reading.
• Be alert while you are reading.
• Stop reading after one or two paragraphs. Ask yourself what you just read. Reread the paragraphs if necessary.
• Relate the information to your personal life. Think of something that happened to you or a friend to help you put the information into a real-world context.
• Use your imagination to visualize, or see, the information as a picture in your mind's eye.

1. _____ is the process of conducting business using electronic means, especially the Internet.

2. The Internet address of a business is called the _____.

3. The _____ makes it illegal for anyone to create an electronic duplicate of a copyrighted work for commercial profit or private financial gain.

4. An encoded message that appears at the end of a contract created online is called a(n) _____.

5. A copyright extends for the creator's life plus _____ years.

6. When a copyright expires, it goes into the _____ where it may be copied by others.

7. A book, CD, or painting is an example of a fixed _____ medium of expression.

8. The area of law that deals with the buying and selling of computers and computer programs is called _____.

Chapter 19

Chapter 19 Cyberlaw and E-Commerce
Section 19.2 Internet Transactions

Test Prep
What to Ask before a Test

Directions Read the tips below. Then take the practice test that follows by circling the letter of the correct answer.

WHAT TO ASK BEFORE A TEST
Before the day of the test, ask your teacher these questions: • What material will be covered on the test? • What type of test will it be: essay, multiple choice, true/false, short answer, or a combination? • How long will I have to complete the test? • Will the test be on the computer or in printed form? • Will the test be open book or closed book? • How much will this test count toward my grade for this class?

1. The process of conducting business using electronic means is called
   a. cybercrime.　　　　　　　　　**c.** e-commerce.
   b. cyberlaw.　　　　　　　　　　**d.** cybertorts.

2. Laws that protect people and businesses that create or invent ideas and products for computers are called
   a. cybercrime law.　　　　　　　**c.** e-commerce law.
   b. cyberprotection law.　　　　　**d.** cybertort law.

3. A distinctive name, word, symbol, image, or slogan used by a business to identify and distinguish its goods from products sold by others is called a
   a. copyright.　　　　　　　　　　**c.** domain name.
   b. patent.　　　　　　　　　　　　**d.** trademark.

4. A property right that inventors can acquire to protect their rights to make, use, and sell their inventions for a number of years is called a
   a. copyright.　　　　　　　　　　**c.** domain name.
   b. patent.　　　　　　　　　　　　**d.** trademark.

5. Legal protection for literary, artistic, and scientific works is called a
   a. copyright.　　　　　　　　　　**c.** domain name.
   b. patent.　　　　　　　　　　　　**d.** trademark.

6. An encoded message that appears at the end of a contract created online is called
   a. a duplicate signature.　　　　　**c.** a digital signature.
   b. a tangible medium of expression.　**d.** identity theft.

Chapter 19 Cyberlaw and E-Commerce
Chapter Content Vocabulary

English Language Arts
Writing

Directions Use at least eight of the words below in a short essay that shows you understand the meanings of the words.

cyberlaw	cybervandalism
cybercrime	cybertort
cybertrespass	cyberdefamation
cyberspoofing	cyberinvasion of privacy
cyberpiracy	e-commerce
cyberblackmail	digital signature
identity theft	domain name

_____

_____

_____

_____

_____

_____

_____

_____

_____

_____

_____

_____

_____

_____

_____

_____

_____

Chapter 19

Chapter 19 Cyberlaw and E-Commerce
Chapter Academic Vocabulary

 English Language Arts
Reading Skills

Directions Match each word in the box below with its definition. Write the letter of the word on the line next to the matching definition.

a. broadcast

b. duplicate

c. infrastructure

d. sabotage

e. simulate

f. tangible

1. _____ to take on the appearance of something

2. _____ the basic installations and facilities that a community relies on

3. _____ able to be touched or felt; real or solid

4. _____ to make an exact copy or copies of

5. _____ any harm done to some effort in order to get it to fail

6. _____ to publish information or images through electronic means

Chapter 20 Marriage and Divorce
Section 20.1 Marriage Laws

 Note Taking

Directions As you read, write notes, facts, and main ideas in the Note Taking column. Write key words and short phrases in the Cues column. Then summarize the section in the Summary box.

Cues	Note Taking
• Prenuptial agreement: legal contract couples make before getting married dealing with property and support issues	**UNDERSTANDING MARRIAGE LAW** • Most states and the federal government define marriage as the legal union of one man and one woman. **TYPES OF MARRIAGE**
• Bigamy: having two spouses at the same time	**PROHIBITED MARRIAGES** • Bigamy and polygamy are crimes in all states. **REQUIREMENTS OF A LEGAL MARRIAGE** • Age requirement:
Summary	
Most states and the federal government define marriage as the union of one man and one woman as husband and wife.	

Chapter 20

Chapter 20 Marriage and Divorce

Section 20.1 Marriage Laws

 Social Studies
Types of Marriage

Directions Different types of marriage are recognized by law. Some types of marriage are strictly forbidden by law. Place the letter of the type of marriage on the line next to its matching example.

a. common-law marriage
b. ceremonial marriage
c. proxy marriage
d. covenant marriage
e. bigamy
f. polygamy
g. consanguinity
h. affinity

EXAMPLES

_____ **1.** Adopted in Arkansas, Arizona, and Louisiana, this type of marriage is an attempt to reduce divorce and protect children. The parties must have counseling before the wedding and during the marriage to solve conflicts.

_____ **2.** Prohibited in almost half the states, this act consists of marrying one's relative by marriage.

_____ **3.** This type of marriage is prohibited by law in every state. It consists of having more than two spouses at the same time.

_____ **4.** In this type of marriage, an agent acts on behalf of the absent party in the event that one or both parties cannot be present for the wedding ceremony.

_____ **5.** This is an informal type of marriage created by the parties themselves. The parties must agree, by words in the present tense, that they are husband and wife.

_____ **6.** Prohibited in every state, this type of marriage consists of having two spouses at the same time.

_____ **7.** Prohibited in some states, this type of marriage consists of marrying one's relative by blood.

_____ **8.** Most states recognize this type of marriage if the parties declare they are married in the presence of a person authorized by law to conduct marriages.

Chapter 20 Marriage and Divorce
Section 20.1 Marriage Laws

Study Skills
Preparing for Final Exams

Directions Finals week can be a stressful time of year. You can reduce your stress level and still score well on your tests. Read the tips below. Then complete the exercise that follows.

PREPARING FOR FINAL EXAMS
• Start studying ahead of time. Do not try to cram an entire semester of material into a day or two before the test.
• Each week, review the material you covered in class. Note the material that you feel is important and may be on the final exam.
• Keep all of your prior tests and quizzes and use them to review for the final exam. An instructor often will use some of the same test material on the final exam.
• During finals week, get plenty of rest. You want to be able to concentrate while studying and while taking the final.
• Organize group study sessions with your classmates. This may help alert you to material that you may have overlooked on your own.
• Finally, do not put too much pressure on yourself to perform well. Remain as relaxed as possible. Remind yourself that you have prepared properly and will do well on all of your final exams.

Complete these steps to better prepare you for finals week.
1. Make a folder for each class you are enrolled in this semester. Write the name of the course in bold on the front cover.
2. In each folder, put the tests and quizzes you have taken thus far. Mark the information that you feel may be on the final exam. Also, make note of any questions you got wrong. Review the correct answers in case they are on the final.
3. Insert several blank sheets of notebook paper. As the semester progresses, write down any information that you feel may be on the final exam. Use these notes while you are studying for your finals.
4. Use these folders to help you prepare for finals. Remember, do not wait until the last minute. Study a little each week so the information stays fresh in your mind.

Chapter 20

Chapter 20 Marriage and Divorce
Section 20.1 Marriage Laws

Test Taking
Short-Answer Tests

Directions Read the tips below. Then take the practice test that follows.

SHORT-ANSWER TEST TIPS
• Prepare by reviewing study sheets or vocabulary exercises your teacher has handed out.
• Use grammatical clues within a statement as hints to the correct answer.
• If you can think of several answers to a question, write them all down if space is provided. A teacher will never penalize you for extra effort.
• If you do not know the answer, guess using common sense. An educated guess may get you some points; a blank answer will surely earn you none!
• Write short, simple sentences. Remember, the test asks for short answers.

1. Most states and the federal government define marriage as _____

   _____.

2. A(n) _____ is a written and signed legal contract couples make before getting married dealing with property and support issues.

3. A(n) _____ is a certificate issued by a government office giving permission to marry.

4. States that continue to allow common-law marriages require that the parties _____

   _____.

5. Persons under the age of 18 can marry only with the _____.

6. _____ is the illegal act of having more than two spouses at the same time.

7. Marriage to relatives by _____ is prohibited by law in some states.

8. The primary obligation of marriage is the duty of the spouses to _____.

Chapter 20 Marriage and Divorce
Section 20.2 Divorce and Its Legal Consequences

 Note Taking

Directions As you read, write notes, facts, and main ideas in the Note Taking
column. Write key words and short phrases in the Cues column. Then summarize
the section in the Summary box.

Cues	Note Taking
• Two common grounds for annulment: duress and fraud	**HOW MARRIAGES END** • Marriages can end in three ways: **GROUNDS FOR DIVORCE** • Adultery is a crime in some states as well as grounds for divorce, but criminal adultery is difficult to prove. **DIVORCE SETTLEMENT** • A legal settlement must be reached by both parties regarding alimony, child custody/support, distribution of marital property.
• Alimony: support paid to one person by the former spouse	

Summary

A marriage comes to an end in one of three ways: the death of a spouse, annulment, or divorce.

Chapter 20

Chapter 20 Marriage and Divorce
Section 20.2 Divorce and Its Legal Consequences

 Reading Comprehension
Matching

Directions The terms in the box below describe ways marriages end, grounds for divorce, and issues of divorce settlement. Match each term with the correct example that follows. Write the term in the space provided. Not all terms will be used.

adultery	legal custody
alcohol or drug addiction	legal separation
alimony	marital property
annulment	no-fault divorce
cruelty	nonsupport
desertion	physical custody

1. A married couple agrees that there is no chance for reconciliation in their marriage and thus seeks this type of divorce. _____

2. Each person's age, income, and financial resources are considered in determining this type of settlement. _____

3. A husband and wife with two children decide to stop living together but remain married for the time being. _____

4. After her husband is violent toward her several times and left her bruised, a wife seeks a divorce on these grounds. _____

5. A husband seeks a divorce after he learns his wife has been having an affair with another man. _____

6. A wife goes to court to seek an end to her marriage on the grounds that she was forced to marry against her will. _____

7. Terry was able to get a divorce on these grounds by proving that Terry's spouse could provide economic support for their family but refused to do so. _____

8. After the divorce, a judge granted both parents the right to make major decisions about their child's health, education, and welfare. However, the child will live with the mother. What type of custody does the mother have? _____ What type of custody do both parents have? _____

Chapter 20 Marriage and Divorce
Section 20.2 Divorce and Its Legal Consequences

 Study Skills
Procrastination

Directions Complete the chart below to find your level of procrastination.
For each statement, place an X under Always, Sometimes, or Never as it applies
to you.

Number	Statement	Always	Sometimes	Never
1	I know what needs to be done, yet I always find something else to do.			
2	I clean my room or do other household chores before studying.			
3	I tell myself that I do my best work under pressure.			
4	I take my books with me with the intention to study but never open them.			
5	I often feel I could have done better on an assignment if I had only spent more time on it.			

If you answered Always or Sometimes to at least three of the five questions, you have a problem with procrastination.

Chapter 20

Chapter 20 Marriage and Divorce

Section 20.2 Divorce and Its Legal Consequences

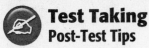 **Test Taking**
Post-Test Tips

Directions Read the tips below. Then take the practice test that follows. Write the correct answer in the space provided.

POST-TEST TIPS
• When you get your corrected test back, always look it over to make sure there are no grading mistakes.
• Look over the test again. If you got any answers wrong, make sure you understand why they were wrong. Do not be afraid to ask another student or your instructor to clarify material you do not understand. This is where the learning comes in.
• Be sure to make note of the questions you answered incorrectly so you can study this material further.
• Save the test for future study. Cumulative final exams often contain questions that are similar to those on previous tests.

1. A(n) _____ is a declaration by the court that a marriage was never valid.
   a. annulment   c. adultery
   b. divorce   d. legal separation

2. Adultery is when one spouse has _____ with someone outside of the marriage.
   a. property   c. sexual relations
   b. rights   d. conversation

3. _____ is an allowance for support paid to one person by the former spouse in a divorce.
   a. Legal custody   c. A prenuptial agreement
   b. Alimony   d. Property

4. _____ deals with which parent the child will live.
   a. Legal custody   c. Child support
   b. Physical custody   d. Child endangerment

5. _____ is the unjustified separation of one spouse from the other with the intent of not returning.
   a. Nonsupport   c. Desertion
   b. Legal separation   d. Cruelty

6. _____ can be grounds for divorce if a spouse can show that there was personal violence that endangered his or her life or health.
   a. Persistence   c. Cruelty
   b. Misconduct   d. Alcohol addiction

Chapter 20 Marriage and Divorce
Chapter Content Vocabulary

English Language Arts
Writing

Directions Use at least eight of the words below in a short essay that shows you understand the meanings of the words.

marriage	affinity
prenuptial agreement	annulment
common-law marriage	divorce
bigamy	adultery
polygamy	no-fault divorce
consanguinity	alimony

_____

_____

_____

_____

_____

_____

_____

_____

_____

_____

_____

_____

_____

_____

_____

Chapter 20

Chapter 20 Marriage and Divorce
Chapter Academic Vocabulary

 English Language Arts
Reading Skills

Directions Use the words in the box below to complete each sentence that follows. Write the word on the line provided.

spouse	persistent
status	reconciliation
ceremony	capacity

1. _____ is the ability to perform or produce.

2. If something never ceases to exist, it is said to be _____.

3. One's partner in marriage is one's _____.

4. A formal event performed on a special occasion is a _____.

5. _____ is the reestablishing of cordial relations.

6. A person's _____ is his or her relative standing in society.

Chapter 20

Chapter 21 Insurance and Estate Planning
Section 21.1 Insurance

 Note Taking

Directions As you read, write notes, facts, and main ideas in the Note Taking column. Write key words and short phrases in the Cues column. Then summarize the section in the Summary box.

Cues	Note Taking
• Policyholder: buyer of insurance policy	**INSURANCE** • Insurance is an agreement in which one party compensates another for any losses.
• Property insurance covers things like cars, homes, and personal items.	**PROPERTY INSURANCE** • Types of property insurance:
	LIFE INSURANCE • Life insurance provides compensation for losses due to a person's death.
	HEALTH INSURANCE • Two major types: basic and major medical

Summary

Insurance compensates people for losses related to:

Chapter 21 Insurance and Estate Planning
Section 21.1 Insurance

Reading Skills
Using a Graphic Organizer

Directions Graphic organizers can help you organize and retain information as you read. Complete the word web by filling in the types of property insurance. Then answer the questions that follow.

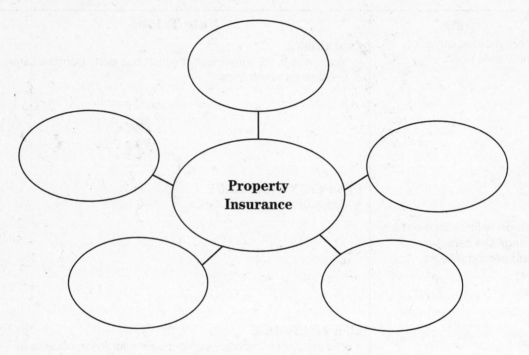

Property Insurance

1. What kind of insurance covers property that is transported?

   _____

2. What kind of insurance is legally required in many states?

   _____

3. What kind of insurance is usually required by mortgage lenders?

   _____

4. What kind of insurance should you carry if you own a home in an area that typically gets heavy rains year round?

   _____

5. What kind of insurance covers damages caused by soot and smoke?

   _____

Chapter 21 Insurance and Estate Planning
Section 21.1 Insurance

 Study Skills
Group Study

Directions Read the tips below. Then write short answers to the questions that follow.

PREPARING FOR GROUP STUDY
• Ask two or three others to study with you. • Schedule enough time for your group to cover all the material. Make sure there is time for questions and discussion. • Select a leader. The leader's task is to keep everyone in the group focused on studying. • Before the group meets, the leader assigns sections of the text to each member. Members should read the entire text, then write questions covering their assigned section. • During the study session, take turns asking and answering one another's questions. If someone cannot answer a question, put it aside to ask again later. • All members of the group should come to the session prepared to answer questions. This will help all of you be prepared for any upcoming class discussion, project, or test. • Plan for a short social time before and after the session. Take at least one short break during the session to rest and clear your minds. The leader should keep track of the time and get everyone focused after a break.

1. Why do you need a group leader?

_____

2. Why should you take short breaks while studying?

_____

_____

_____

3. Why is it important for everyone to be prepared to answer questions before the group meets?

_____

_____

4. What tips would you give to someone who wanted to organize a study group?

_____

_____

_____

Chapter 21 Insurance and Estate Planning
Section 21.1 Insurance

 Test Taking
Fill-in-the-Blank Tests

Directions Practice the tips below while taking the practice test that follows.
Fill in the blank with the best word choice from the list.

TAKING FILL-IN-THE-BLANK TESTS
• Carefully read each statement before answering. Think about what each word means.
• Read the statement again.
• Fill in the statements you are sure of with the best word choice. Some words may be close in meaning to others, so make sure you choose the best one.
• Cross out each word as you use it.
• Once you have eliminated the words you are sure of, go back over the words you are less sure of and reread each statement. Fill in the blank with the best remaining choice.
• Check your answers.
• Reread all the statements to make sure you have answered each one.

term life	endowment
policyholder	Medicare
marine	annuity

1. The buyer of an insurance policy is called a(n) _____.

2. _____ policies are typically written for periods of 10, 20, or 30 years.

3. Today, ocean _____ insurance covers goods shipped at sea.

4. A(n) _____ is a guaranteed retirement income that may be purchased by paying a lump-sum premium.

5. _____ insurance is the least expensive because it has no cash or loan value.

6. _____ is a federally funded health insurance program for people who are covered by Social Security.

Chapter 21 Insurance and Estate Planning
Section 21.2 Estate Planning

 Note Taking

Directions As you read, write notes, facts, and main ideas in the Note Taking column. Write key words and short phrases in the Clues column. Then summarize the section in the Summary box.

Clues	Note Taking
• IRA = Individual Retirement Account	**ESTATE PLANNING** • Estate planning assures your assets remain intact to protect your family before and after death.
• Testator/testatrix:	**WILLS** • Will: document signed during your lifetime that provides for the distribution of your property upon death • Wills must meet certain requirements:
• Trustee:	**TRUSTS** • Trust:

Summary
Estate planning is the process of assuring that a person's assets remain intact to protect the family before or after death. Estate planning includes:

Chapter 21 Insurance and Estate Planning

Section 21.2 Estate Planning

 Reading Comprehension
Reading a Table

Directions The table below shows what would happen to your estate if you died without a will in the state of Massachusetts. Use it to answer the questions that follow.

INTESTATE SUCCESSION	
If you are survived by:	**Your estate is distributed:**
1. Spouse and child(ren)	One half to spouse, one half to children
2. Spouse, no children, but next of kin (including parents, siblings, niece, nephew, aunt, uncle, cousin, etc.)	Where the estate is less than $200,000, all to spouse. If the estate is larger than $200,000, the first $200,000 plus one half of everything in excess of $200,000 to spouse. The remainder to next of kin in this order: parent(s), siblings, nieces and nephews, grandparents, uncles and aunts, cousins.
3. Spouse, no child, no next of kin	All to spouse
4. No spouse, one or more children	All to children
5. No spouse, no child, but next of kin	All to next of kin, in the order described above in 2.
6. No spouse, no child, no next of kin	All escheats to the state, that is, all turned over to the state because there are no heirs or beneficiaries.

Source: Massachusetts Law of Descent and Distribution Law of Intestate Succession (G.L. c. 190 §1)

1. If you died in Massachusetts, how would your estate be distributed if you had no spouse but one or more children?

_____

2. If your estate was less than $200,000 and you died with a spouse and next of kin but no children, how would your estate be distributed?

_____

3. Who are first in the line of succession for next of kin?

_____

4. What does *escheats* mean?

_____

5. How would your estate be distributed if you had a spouse and one or more children?

_____

Chapter 21 Insurance and Estate Planning
Section 21.2 Estate Planning

Study Skills
Planning Study Time

Directions Read the tips below. Then answer the questions that follow.

TIPS FOR PLANNING STUDY TIME
• Planning out your time will actually result in more time to study, because you will be using your time more effectively.
• Write down all your tasks and activities for one week; for example, going to class, studying, after-school practice, chores, and sleeping.
• Record the hours you spend studying, in class, with your family, with friends, participating in sports, playing a musical instrument, sleeping, grooming, and so on. Include the time you use for relaxing. Time to relax is important so you can refresh yourself and clear your mind.
• Make a scheduling calendar. Use different colors to create blocks of time. For example, yellow for time in school and red for time with your friends.
• Look at your calendar. Are there any time conflicts? Are there blocks of time where you have too many activities and other blocks where you have nothing at all? Try to strike a balance by rearranging your schedule.
• Change your schedule as activities in your life change. For example, you may want to schedule more time for studying a week or two before a test.

1. How does planning your time help you study?

_____

_____

2. How might using different colors help you with your schedule?

_____

_____

3. Why should you plan time to relax and do things you enjoy?

_____

_____

4. Why might you need to revise your schedule?

_____

5. On average, how much time do you think you should schedule for studying each week? Explain your answer.

_____

_____

Chapter 21 Insurance and Estate Planning
Section 21.2 Estate Planning

 Test Taking
Test-Taking Tips

Directions Read the tips below. Then take the practice test that follows.

TEST-TAKING TIPS

- Skip questions you are stuck on and come back to them later. You just might come up with the answer while working on another part of the test.
- If you are not sure of the full answer, answer as much as you can. You might get partial credit.
- Once you have written an answer, move on to the next question. Do not waste time editing or rewriting your answer. If you have time at the end of the test, then you can go back and edit your answers.
- Write clearly. That is, make sure both your handwriting and your ideas are clear.

1. Why is it important to start a retirement plan early?

_____

_____

2. Who can make a will?

_____

_____

3. To be valid, a will must be attested. What does *attested* mean?

_____

_____

4. What is a living will?

_____

_____

5. What type of trust is usually set up by parents to provide for their own children?

_____

_____

6. What does the homestead exemption do?

_____

_____

Chapter 21 Insurance and Estate Planning
Chapter Content Vocabulary

 English Language Arts
Definitions

Directions Write the correct word on the line next to its definition.

insurance	term life insurance	intestate
premium	will	probate
beneficiary	testator/testatrix	executor/executrix
insurable interest	testamentary intent	trust
straight life insurance	testamentary capacity	trustee

1. _____ The process of validating and executing a will.

2. _____ An agreement in which one party compensates another party for any losses.

3. _____ Life insurance that requires the payment of premiums until the face value is reached or the insured is deceased.

4. _____ A person who dies with a will.

5. _____ To be without a will.

6. _____ The intention that the document is meant to be a last will and testament.

7. _____ The person named to carry out the terms of a will.

8. _____ A legal device by which property is held by one person for the benefit of another.

9. _____ A person who holds title to the property for another's benefit.

10. _____ Life insurance issued for a particular period, usually five or ten years.

11. _____ The person named in an insurance policy to receive the proceeds.

12. _____ The financial interest a policyholder has in the person or property that is insured and would suffer from the loss of.

13. _____ The mental ability (being of sound mind) to create a will.

14. _____ A document that is signed during your lifetime that provides for the distribution of your property upon death.

15. _____ The amount of money an insured pays for insurance coverage.

Chapter 21 Insurance and Estate Planning
Chapter Academic Vocabulary

 English Language Arts
Reading Skills

Directions Use the academic vocabulary words to create a word-search puzzle like the one below. Carefully write each word in the squares of the grid, one letter per box. Arrange the words going up, down, across, diagonally, or backward. Fill in the remaining squares with random letters. When you are finished, exchange puzzles with a classmate and solve each other's puzzle.

comprehensive   routine   elective
endowment   supplement   directive

e	w	r	t	p	p	t	e	v	i	t	c	e	l	e
d	i	r	e	t	y	p	a	k	j	c	e	n	o	l
c	o	m	p	s	u	p	b	v	d	z	t	d	y	u
o	e	p	h	a	g	i	r	e	s	l	k	j	u	t
m	n	a	s	d	d	f	u	s	t	c	k	r	l	p
a	d	i	r	e	c	i	b	s	o	e	r	o	s	w
p	o	g	h	y	t	r	r	e	d	s	q	u	n	j
r	w	a	s	u	p	p	l	e	m	e	n	t	e	m
s	m	i	t	t	s	d	a	g	c	e	w	i	k	o
a	e	q	w	e	r	t	y	u	i	t	o	n	p	l
e	n	d	o	w	y	g	h	o	t	y	i	e	n	a
d	t	o	f	f	k	l	e	r	v	b	a	v	s	s
s	c	o	m	p	r	e	h	e	n	s	i	v	e	r
a	s	d	f	g	g	j	u	k	l	o	p	e	a	t
v	b	n	o	p	i	e	w	c	v	b	e	t	y	i

Puzzles will vary. All six vocabulary words must be used.

Notes

Notes

Notes

Notes

Notes

Notes

Notes

Notes